Focus
for
Success

Focus for Success

A Primer for Entrepreneurs and Business People

BY JAMES A. EITING
Chair, Midmark Corporation

ORANGE FRAZER PRESS
Wilmington, Ohio

ISBN 978-1933197-623
Copyright © 2009 James A. Eiting

Copies of *Focus for Success: A Primer for Entrepreneurs and Business People* may be ordered directly from:

Midmark Corporation
60 Vista Drive, PO Box 286
Versailles, OH 45380
937.526.8303
www.midmark.com

"The Man in the Glass" originally titled "The Guy in the Glass" copyright ©1934, Peter "Dale" Wimbrow, Sr.

Design by Chad DeBoard

Library of Congress Cataloging-in-Publication Data

Eiting, James A. (James August), 1936-
  Focus for success : a primer for entrepreneurs and business people / by James A. Eiting.
      p. cm.
  ISBN 978-1-933197-62-3 (alk. paper)
  1. Small business--Management. 2. Success in business. 3. Entrepreneurship. I. Title.
  HD62.7.E394 2009
  658.4'09--dc22
                                    2009003684

DEDICATED *to*

My loving wife Esther of many years, our children and grand-children, and the entrepreneurial spirit we hope they carry on in a way that fits their lifestyles. May this book be a stepping stone in their efforts to help mankind.

TABLE *of* CONTENTS

PART SIX: THE ESSENTIALS

PART SEVEN: PHILOSOPHICAL THINKING

PART EIGHT: THE FUTURE

PART NINE: SUNSET

I would like to ACKNOWLEDGE...

that I have been blessed with so many wonderful mentors and advisors, I have decided not to try to name them all. They know who they are and I am hopeful some of them will see themselves as they read this book.

Thank you to Dr. Anne Eiting Klamar, CEO of Midmark, from whom I have learned so much, as well as to our entire board of directors for their very strong support of the project. My thanks to Olive Tumbusch, who skillfully typed my first manuscript from longhand and then took it into a second manuscript form.

Thank you to Carolyn Porter and Alan Gadney of One-on-One, book shepherds who advised me through the first incarnation of this book. Finally, our public relations department suggested Orange Frazer Press in Wilmington, Ohio. I work well with Marcy Hawley and I thank them for their editorial and design expertise, and for getting this book into its final form.

I appreciate all the people who were kind enough to read the initial chapters and for their advice on how to make them better (which confirms my marketing mind).

Finally, all the challenges life has brought me. They have been necessary ingredients for success.

A *little* BACKGROUND MUSIC

Willie Eiting in Germany

One November many years ago, I had to be in Hamburg, Germany, on business and my trip there ended on a Friday. So Saturday morning I rented a car and drove to Bocholt, a place I had read that Eitings had lived in the early 1700s. I had learned of it through a funeral card in Decatur, Indiana.

It was a dreary northern Germany day and it was a four-hour drive to Bocholt. As I got close, I stopped at a phone booth and found to my surprise a few Eitings listed. I was very excited even though I had no idea who to contact. (What I thought to be a village of 2,500, was actually a town of 70,000—a stone's throw from the Holland border.)

Since it was off the beaten path, I could not find anyone who spoke English, and I had no hotel reservation. It was getting dark and I couldn't even find a hotel. Such moments will give you religion.

Naturally, I was a bit lost and as I was driving down a side street in somewhat of a panic, I came across a sign that said, "Eiting Hotel and Restaurant Two Blocks." I stopped, put my head on the steering wheel and said out loud, "Thank you, God."

I went the two blocks, parked and locked the car, then walked into the restaurant. There behind the bar, wiping a beer glass, was a man who looked like a twin of my grandfather whom I had never met as he had died the year before I was born. I tried to explain who I was: "Eiting. America, 150 years." Neither of us was fluent in each other's language, but he smiled, turned around, and tapped me a beer.

Of course I asked for a room. That night, there was a band and the restaurant fed me like royalty. In the morning I was given a wonderful breakfast. When it came time to check out, I asked for a bill and directions to St. George's Church. They would not accept any payment, so I went off to 11 a.m. mass. I had tears in my eyes as I thought of all the Eiting baptisms, marriages, and funerals that had likely taken place there.

Am I too emotional? Perhaps, but don't forget this was the first family contact in 150 years. It was a powerful moment indeed. And, to find Eitings as mercantile people in the old country was very confirming.

I have always felt that perhaps at the time of the Crusades or the Reformation that our family had morphed over from Judaism to Christianity. Of course, in the time before Christ, Judaism was the only religion of one god. I have always respected people of the Jewish faith and have admired their approach to life. I always felt that in a former life I was a Jewish violinist in Budapest, but in going to Budapest it did not feel *right* to me. When we went on to Prague and to the Jewish cemetery down by the river, I just *melted*, feeling a *very* strong attraction there, thinking we must have ancestors buried there (thus, my passion for cabbage, accordion and violin music. So much for conjecture.)

My great grandfather came to America with his siblings in 1849. He had a general store in the village of Minster, Ohio. I feel the reason they ended up there is because it is flat like northern Germany with similar, extremely fertile soil. The Minster village to this day is probably 95 percent German and also 95 percent Catholic. It's a very nice town. I distinctly remember my parents and grandparents speaking low German, and classmates from the area farms being more fluent in low German than English.

As a child I saw an abandoned brick building with a sign that read, "Minster Woolen Mill, J. Eiting & Sons." That always made me feel special. Notable too, Bocholt was the weaving area of Germany.

Minster Woolen Mill—J. Eiting, 1875

The owner of the mill was named Johann and his son was named John. John married into a somewhat wealthy family. They owned a machinery company called The Minster Machine Company, and my grandfather John, an investor, eventually became secretary/treasurer of that machine company. Later, he was also secretary/treasurer of three other companies and a board member of another machinery company and a bank (which he organized with other people's capital when he was only 38 years old).

He was also on the board of a cannery, a foundry, a brewery, a telephone company and a mutual insurance company. Finally, although his full-time job was at the Minster Machine Company he eventually became president of the Cummings Machine Company. He never took a dominant shareholder position in anything (more on this later).

I suppose the capstone of his economic prowess was starting the Minster State Bank in 1914. It is one of the few banks that went through the Depression unscathed and is highly successful and independent to this day. His wife (my grandmother) liked to say, "We are just a little pickle in a big jar."

The Cummings Machine Company (predecessor of Midmark) was started in 1915 to build concrete mixers. It eventually made small gauge switch engines and ultimately became the Industrial Equipment Company in 1921. At that point they were basically a steel fabricator.

My father, Carl, who graduated from Xavier University in 1928, joined the Industrial Equipment Company in purchasing and remained in that job until 1953 when he was elected president. His father died in May of 1935 and my father was elected

Carl Eiting, kneeling far left, 1938.

secretary/ treasurer and board member at that time.

I graduated from the University of Dayton in 1956 with a two-year degree in industrial engineering. Perhaps the only thing I wanted to do was get out of school and go to work—anywhere. I wanted to join Sandia Corporation in Albuquerque, New Mexico, but in my last year of college, my father suffered a second heart attack and my mother was pretty insistent that I help my dad. We always had a wonderful relationship until he died in 1972. My sister's husband, Frank Brinkman, had also joined the company, taking over my father's purchasing spot and becoming treasurer. He retired in 1984, and he passed away in 2000. We always had a fine relationship.

My brother, following his graduation, joined the other machine company mentioned, which made metal processing equipment for steel mills, etc. He left them in the '70s and started his own metal processing company which, today, has eight plants in four states. I am very proud of his robust success. He sold the company in 2004.

My other sister's husband eventually ended up in Denver and started a very successful electronics company which has gone public. My sister is an artist and we are the best of friends. Her husband, Luke, worked his way through Ohio State University by painting flag poles.

So, among the three remaining males, there are three fairly robust and productive companies, which is unusual considering they are entirely independent of each other (our family members, male and female, are very independent). We often say, "We have two settings—off and wide open."

From the left: Marie and Jack Eiting, my sister Judy and her husband Luke, Esther and me, and my sister Janice.

So this is a *snapshot* of me, born too late to know my grandfather, with whom I would have loved to have sat and talked, as he had to have organizational and economic brilliance.

I was fortunate to grow up in the shadow of the Depression and experience the rationing of World War II. These were wonderful experiences for me and tended to make one very prudent. Like someone said, "We were so poor growing up, we never got to sleep alone until after we were married!" Looking back on World War II, lectures about turning out the lights and not using too much hot water (bath on Saturday night only) was really good for a child. I also remember walking to school in my five-buckle Arctics and seeing the dirt from the coal smoke that makes the snow brown. On Sundays, I went to church wearing my brother's hand-me-down knickers. Milk was delivered to our door in glass bottles and television was nowhere to be seen. I often think that all the Monopoly and chess we played really sharpened our business skills.

Following my graduation in 1956, I was working in the engineering department at the Industrial Equipment Company. Their sales volume was $500,000. I saw that there was very little sales effort and thus volunteered to go on the road. I married in early 1957, and Esther turned out to be a great wife and mother and a real corporate supporter. So, there I was, out of college, married, on the road and not yet 21. Esther and I like to think we raised each other, as she was just 19.

I had four percent of the company stock given to me by my father. The company had fifty employees and still paid employees with cash in the 1950s. There was not even an organization chart. My territory was from upstate New York to Wisconsin. Well, I'm pleased to say that, due to some great people, we did fairly well. I also quickly spotted that we could never be better than our customers, because our meager existence depended on their success. We had to re-prove ourselves every day.

However, I realize that I had some great mentors who really helped me along the way. As a result, I ended up (over the years) on about ten corporate boards, which gave me experience in machinery, foundries, and banking, to name a few. I was very fortunate to be able to include many years with the Young Presidents Organization—an incredible experience, and I soaked it all up like a sponge.

From the day I started at the Industrial Equipment Company, the people there kept saying, "We need a product of our own!" Therefore, in 1967, when I was named general manager, I concluded we would take our skills and market them in a different direction with a product of our own. I decided our product would be either institutional feeding equipment (i.e. cafeteria stainless steel, etc.) or medical equipment. The medical equipment idea was based on demographics and it being recession-resistant, and I liked it best because I always felt there are riches in niches.

From a medical dealer in Cincinnati, I learned that a medical table company in North Vernon, Indiana, American Metal

Furniture Co., had just closed its doors. I also found out that it was owned by a company in Winchester, Indiana, only fifty miles away from our company. After thinking it over for a few days, I approached my father and brother-in-law, Frank Brinkman, and they backed me up. We called the parent company, Overmyer Mould Company, and eventually worked up to a price of $30,000 and they agreed to finance the purchase at six percent interest. This was basically for the name and the drawings. Luckily, I was too young and dumb to be afraid. Everything we bought was loaded onto a pickup truck and moved to an old furniture store we had bought in anticipation of this acquisition.

There will be less use of the word "I" because it was a team effort by hard-working, spirited and smart young people. I'm forever grateful to them as they were very helpful as we learned and grew up together. We actually and unwittingly motivated and mentored each other.

The following is a summation of what we learned along the way.

PREFACE

George Burns once said, "The secret of a good sermon is to have a good opening and a good ending and have the two as close together as possible." Thus I have written a short, concise book.

Perhaps you will only find useful five or six ideas presented here. If so, the book will still be well worth the read. The same goes if it validates what you already know. I am a firm believer in Pareto's Principle of the 80/20. Twenty percent of you may not find the book useful. That's okay. I want to help the 80 percent who do, become more successful.

There are hundreds of books written on the subject of business and business principles (about 1200/year). I feel this is one of the few with an abridged style. It is a primer for the ambitious person who has found himself or herself in need of business mentoring. My seminal theme? —To help you be more successful and not make the many mistakes I have made in my career.

I began making notes for the book during my travels over the last quarter century. I started it in long hand, and through the years I have found it to be a great guide for me as I mentored people.

Finally, Warren Buffett, who turned over millions of dollars to the Bill and Melinda Gates Foundation, gave them only one piece of advice: STAY FOCUSED!

Focus for Success

PART ONE:
THE HUNT

Opportunities

Opportunities are fleeting. Their intensity changes by the minute, the hour, the month, and the year. Be vigilant and seize them...*now!*

When I was made general manager, the person who I believed to be the best president and leader in our area, Jim Dicke, Sr., the president of Crown Equipment, asked me to join him on our Selective Service Board at the county seat. This was during the Vietnam War. Since my father was *our* company's president, I asked him what he thought I should do. His advice was, "No." I went ahead and joined the board anyway, as it was thirty minutes to the county seat and the meetings were monthly. This gave me twelve hours of mentoring time with this person every year. This choice was extremely successful for me.

Every success creates new opportunities, but then, so does every failure! Ironically, failure is a *very* important ingredient of success!

Richard P. Carlton, former CEO of 3M once said: "We have indeed stumbled into some of our new products, but remember, you can only stumble if you are moving." When someone says, "It can't be done," it's a beacon for opportunity. Breaking the rules can also create opportunity.

In the book *Celestine Prophecy*, it says, "Look for signs." I consistently do, and find that when I get more than one sign, it's a good idea or a "go ahead." It's a *trigger point* for me. And when I see four or five signs, it's a *go*.

If you're looking for a totally *new* market, target an organization that has had a very high market share for generations. Chances are they may be fat and happy and thus sloppy with their costs. Usually, they are slow to take action because they don't know how!

Finally, look for a niche market. These are overlooked portions of markets that are being missed by the big guys. That's where market segmentation comes into play. High-market-share people convince themselves that one size fits all, and it never does. Therefore, many times the niches end up being opportunities for you to segue into a new market.

Buying & Selling

One of the reasons Midmark has had a robust balance sheet is that we taught ourselves to be good buyers. There is an expression, "well bought is half sold," which means you make your seminal profit move when you *buy*.

And, when buying, there is a great question to ask: "Is there anything that I should know that you haven't told me?" Then, wait at least twenty-four hours before signing on the dotted line. (Caveat emptor.)

Of course, the best time to *sell* is when you have a buyer. (For example, you are under no pressure to lower your price.) Once the strike price is agreed upon, make your move.

During my wonderful experience as a partner with three venture capital groups, Hastings Equity and Metapoint Partners, in Boston, and American Securities, in New York, we have owned many, many companies. And, unless they are clinkers, I often fall in love with them and do not want to sell. This can be the wrong approach. So, stay ahead of the curve, whether you are selling a company, a stock, a home, or whatever. The logic is, you are certain of today, but not of tomorrow. Never try to sell at what you think will be the top price. When Baron Rothschild was asked how he got rich, he said, "By always selling too soon."

You'll make your greatest gain in buying when there is blood running in the streets. Generally, something that can be bought cheaply (that's been up for sale a long time) is hard to sell at a higher price. But you can change the equation by investing intelligently. One might buy a home that is close to deterioration but has "good bones" and is in a "turnaround" neighborhood. If you have a vision of what it can become and you don't mind hard work, buying and reselling can be a fun game. Historically, we have profited from homes we have owned. But when it's time to sell, don't overprice— you'll lose your audience very quickly. Our homes always sold quickly because we were not greedy. We priced them fairly and they sold quickly (see Value chapter). And our very personal added value has been my wife and partner, Esther, who has maintained our homes to perfection.

Ask yourself, "Am I buying a problem or an opportunity?" Planning and forethought provide the biggest return on a purchase. Think it through. Remember, it's the *second* mouse that ends up getting the cheese from the trap…

Acquisitions

Midmark has made acquisitions of varying sizes. Most were not product extensions for us. We are constantly looking for them, finding that, the bigger the deal, the bigger the risk. This is where having a vision really counts. Is the potential acquisition a strategic decision? What are the potential benefits? One of our most interesting transactions we made was with a stretcher company based in Maryland. It was owned by one of our West Coast distributors. Since we had little money, we just kept shipping them product at no charge (which they were already selling), until their company was eventually paid for—by us.

A *good* acquisition has good people who will remain with the business to share the knowledge they have within them. Intellectual capital is always the game, and many times the true leader is buried in the second tier of people. Remember that a company's balance sheet and profit and loss (P&L) sheet may be insignificant compared to the intellectual capital you hope to acquire.

Often, your cheapest acquisition can end up being the most expensive. One reason a company may be inexpensive is that the venture capital people have already looked them over and declined to purchase. Therefore, you had better check them over *very* thoroughly. We once bought a company with a highly technical product. When we looked at their inventory, every box was there, but eighty percent of them were filled with products that were rejects. That company was for sale for a reason. Always look under the hood, carefully and slowly. Caveat emptor.

Make certain you have a merger and acquisition specialist with whom you have worked and are comfortable. This person will save you their fee many times over if they are good. We have one. When a friend of mine was unsuccessful in trying to acquire a company, we put him in touch with our specialist. But my friend felt that he was too expensive and, of course, as a result, he did not acquire the company. An *inexpensive* acquisition specialist can be the *most expensive* in the long run.

We recently lost an acquisition because we felt it carried too much bad baggage. They insisted that we accept their liabilities. We refused because we wanted to buy opportunity, not problems. Their technology and product should be current and not dated. When you buy or hire a problem, you not only lose time and money in correcting it, you lose time better used for other opportunities. Lost opportunity is expensive. Acquisitions are about collapsing time, and using that time to move forward.

A key acquisition question is, "How deep is the management?" If it is deep, you can well afford to pay a high EBITA (Earnings Before Income Tax & Amortization) multiple. A smart attorney who specialized in Mergers and Acquisitions (M&A) work told me that the value is the same with or without the real estate. It all gets down to strategic benefits.

Still another key ingredient in acquisition strategy is competitor analysis. Properly done, it should lead you to the targeted acquisitions, with laser accuracy. With deep financial analysis of the target, you may find you can afford to pay a very steep EBITA multiple, especially if it is "strategic."

When acquiring a company, you don't have to know *every* detail, but you had better understand the big picture (the gestalt). If the company is strategic, is focused, and if the compatibility is there, even if you're overpaying, in ten years you'll declare it a bargain.

Finally, do you have a contingent exit strategy going in? If not, create one immediately. If the acquisition looks rough around the edges, can it be fixed, and at what cost? Factor that into the offer. Eighty percent of the time, people will only see the benefits of an acquisition and ignore the potential problems. Always have an exit strategy before you buy. Will Rogers said it this way: "Letting the cat out of the bag is a whole lot easier 'n puttin' it back in."

Entrepreneurs

We are largely a nation of immigrants, and immigration takes a lot of guts! It's likely that somewhere in our ancestry is someone who sailed across the sea with a one-way ticket and no guarantees except a chance to improve their financial lot. They not only risked their capital to get here, but their lives, as well.

I am a part-time resident of California and I'm included in entrepreneurship at the university level there, as well as in the Midwest. I have always felt this: The first immigrants settled on the East Coast and started careers in such diverse businesses as ship's chandlers, bankers, or insurance, and dozens more. Many in the second wave of immigration moved into the vast Midwest and cleared the forests, tilled the rich soil, and became farmers and innovative business people, in order to survive. This was not possible in Europe.

Other risk-takers made it all the way to the West Coast, began businesses, and had to become even more innovative. They developed vast irrigation systems and dams. (Because of their boldness and creativity, I feel that's the reason Californians make so many product breakthroughs in fields such as computer hardware and software. When I was a young man, new ideas seemed to begin on the East Coast and move westward. Today, it seems like things start in California and move eastward around the entire globe.)

Many of these immigrants were America's first entrepreneurs. But entrepreneurs are not *always* the risk-takers you might think they are. Though they are not afraid of risk, they are usually very logical and disciplined thinkers and enjoy control. They do their homework and are hands-on. And although money is part of the objective, it is often only to keep score. The real objective is for the entrepreneur to have fun chasing a vision that has appeared in his or her mind. They see opportunity where others just see risk.

Often, entrepreneurs can be impulsive. An entrepreneur might just get his or her organization up and running when it's spotted by a big organization (such as Microsoft, Johnson & Johnson, etc.)

that recognizes potential. They are so flattered to be recognized by "Mr. Big," that too many times they'll end up selling, only to be disappointed later. The money is there, but the challenge is gone. And money is not an end in itself, but a means to an end. Personally, I know many people who have sold their companies and very few are happy.

We were once approached by "Mr. Big," and flattered to be courted by a billion dollar organization. Fortunately, we had the resolve and maturity to turn them down. Remember, big organizations, by and large, get big by acquiring entrepreneurs who had a better idea.

Entrepreneurs, generally, do not like rules, restrictions, or organizations that become too large. But, they can run into trouble because their organization lacks the discipline of more established, larger companies. They find that they either must sell, perhaps because of weak P&Ls or balance sheets, or out of sheer frustration. Their size precludes making every decision themselves the way they used to do. From a purely emotional standpoint, it is easier to start a business than to get out of it.

Entrepreneurs do have some advantages. They start fresh, without too much doubt. With their hands on every aspect, they see their company being built one brick at a time and truly understand what's going on every day. John A Gartner, a psychologist from Johns Hopkins University, when writing for *Worth* magazine, said, "The U.S. makes up only five percent of the world's population, but 25 percent of its economic activity."

A final thought: I believe entrepreneurs are, in general, generous. More so than those who inherited their wealth. Is this because the entrepreneur figures he or she can make it again if necessary and the inherited wealthy are simply afraid to lose what they've been given? I don't know for sure. "In the end," a Jewish proverb states, "life is the greatest bargain. We get it for nothing."

PART TWO: CASH IS KING

Investments

Your goal should always be to use the money made by investments so that you can use the acquired money instead of yours. If *your* money is safe, you can *really* afford risk.

Get rich slowly. There will be less pressure, you'll enjoy life more, and you'll sleep better. Besides, when you hit 60, your goal will be to *zero out* or you'll have to be in a rush again at the end of your life!

Cash is king and always will be. It gives you flexibility. Therefore, invest in things that can be easily converted to cash.

If you inherited some asset or security or lucked out on an inexpensive purchase, your yield is now essentially exponential because your initial investment was so very little. Think of that before you sell a long-held asset. In selling, you must pay a capital gains tax, and you also have the risk of poor re-investment.

Buy when there is blood running in the streets. You want to be buying when others are selling and vice-versa. It takes tremendous courage to do that, but your greatest increments of profit will be made that way. Most people invest in something after it is a winner, and they pay dearly for it. The key is to get there before it is a winner and buy at low prices. That's where you'll need clairvoyance. I always feel you make your big profit when you *buy* rather than *sell*. If your bet is right, it gives you instant conviction and allows you to quickly work with their capital rather than yours.

Never try to time the market. Think only in terms of three to five years. Checking the price of a security every three months is quite adequate. This is assuming you own only high quality securities. Remember, too, it is not a stock market, but a market of stocks.

I have learned that the most important ingredient in an investment is the quality, honesty and background of its leader. Typically, I did quite well when Jack Welch stepped down at G.E. I just followed where the people went who wanted, but didn't get, his job. They were really heavyweights.

The most essential way to a good return is to keep from losing it in the first place. Preservation of capital is Rule Number One. Said Will Rogers, "I'm not so much concerned with a return on my capital but a return *of* it!"

This final note on investments. The easiest way to make a profit is to be clever, though honest, with taxes. Teach yourself to harvest your losses. Losses *do* have value, if you plan.

Financial

In 1971, I spent a short amount of time at the Harvard Business School and I learned four things while there: 1. I wasn't as smart as I thought I was. (This is a great lesson in itself.); 2. If you read something great about a stock in *Forbes, Fortune,* etc., you might almost sell it short as it has possibly been on the cocktail circuit in New York City for *at least* three days; 3. Look at the balance sheet before the profit and loss sheet. It is the soul of a company; 4. If you're going to bet, bet on yourself, as you're fairly certain of the outcome if you work hard.

To begin with, learn that cash is king and always will be. I used to think owning assets was smart and it certainly is not dumb. However, if you can, lease and conserve your cash so you're flexible and can move fast when opportunities in your core business present themselves. Besides, at the end of the lease, disposal of the item leased is their probelm, not yours. Cash in inventory, receivables, and plant and equipment won't enable you to move fast to close an acquisition or raise cash. Inventory and receivables must be kept lean. Although cash *should be your least* productive asset, we always felt much more comfortable with it than without it. In the final analysis, free cash flow is always the name of the game (cash from operations, including depreciation, minus capital expenditures). That is the soul of any operation. Earnings can be an opinion. Cash is a fact!

One day, our president was looking at an acquisition she felt to be overpriced. At the same time, I was on the board of an organization that the banks were beginning to crowd. Our organization had a lot of cash at that moment and I commented, "You can afford to pay top dollar because your money is worth much less in terms of utility than the money of the organization the bank is concerned about." The value of money (cash) is different in different situations.

Soon after I was called back to the organization from retirement, our daughter, Anne Eiting-Klamar, M.D., was elected president, making her the fourth-generation of the Eiting family to hold a leadership position. She struggled and re-struggled to get our costs back into line. She finally looked at *every* non-production invoice and also put everyone, including myself, on a tight budget. It worked and she swung the company back to its former financial prowess within twenty-four months. A typical example was thumping two V.P.s for having dinner together at Morton's in Chicago. Called on the carpet, they were told that Morton's was only to be used with a customer, and pizza would do when without one!

Looking at numbers is important. Knowing what's in the costs is more so! Knowing and correctly assigning your costs are bedrock when it comes to running a successful business. And don't do it in a cursory fashion. Have your controller and staff spend time on your plant floors and dig, dig, dig for costs. Then assign them. Of course, curb wasteful spending. An organization that doesn't accurately know its costs is out of control. Your chief financial officer's (CFO) job should be reporting costs, but cost cutting should precede that. Luckily, that is a skill set which transfers to a new company rather easily. A weak CFO is an expensive CFO.

Another important financial lesson is learning how to price your merchandise. Price your product according to competition and not your costs, as many times costs are wrong. And, make sure your customer is paying for every feature and service included with your product.

Here is a very personal note on pricing, because *I* was the product. For years, I spoke at meetings, conventions, and universities. When I realized I really had something of value, I began to charge for my speaking engagements, starting with $250, then $500, finally $1,000, unless it was a school. An acquaintance of mine convinced me that it was worth more. So, I went to $2,000…and stopped getting calls. Thus, the true value was $1,000. In other words, compare your value with your information and the going rate.

A good financial lesson to learn is that it's much tougher to fix a balance sheet than a P&L sheet. If we think of an organization as a person, the legs are its facilities, the arms are its product, and the head is its people, the spine, then, is its balance sheet. Weak spines can't stand straight, and without a strong one, the body could collapse. Show me a strong balance sheet and I'll show you a strong core of people; conversely a weak one is the result of undisciplined people.

Last, in terms of an easy yield, tax planning has the greatest return of all. Think ahead!

In the end, here are some important thoughts to remember:

- Creditors have much better memories than debtors. They are better to have than shareholders.
- It's better to pay interest than taxes. Besides, the tension that that creates is good for an organization.
- "Figures don't lie, but liars figure"—never, ever forget that! I learned that lesson many times!
- When a fellow says, "It's not the money but the principle of the thing," ...it's the money!
- Anyone who thinks money will make you happy, hasn't got money.
- Teach yourself to spot value. Many times you'll have to go against the tide to do so. You must be confident in yourself and your logic to see *intrinsic* value where others do not. So *believe and bet on yourself* and *your* logic, even though it seems that, sometimes, you're throwing sand against the tide.

Finally, this on pricing from *Fortune* magazine. "McKinsey research finds that in a typical S&P 500 company, a price cut of 5% would have to generate increased sales volume of 19% in order to pay for itself—and that almost never happens. The implication is that while holding prices steady may cause sales to decline somewhat, that course may nonetheless be wiser."

PART THREE: GOVERNANCE

Being a Corporate Director

When asked to join a corporate board, this is the absolute first question to investigate:

- "Is the integrity there?" It must be flawless, as you don't need another problem.
- If it passes this first test, then question two is, "Will my experience and background bring something to the party?"
- And question three is, "Will I learn from the experience?"
- Question four is, "Are you being asked only because your name brings prestige to the board or to stroke the ego of the owners?"

When asked to join a board, use the same caution you would upon entering a new business. Carefully look at the balance sheet, the market share, the work ethic of the top people, their intelligence, and their reputation.

The role of a good corporate director is to ask questions—the deeper the better. And, don't be satisfied with a quick fabricated answer. Your reputation is at stake as well!

When I was on different audit committees, my last question always was, "Is there anything we should know that you haven't told us?"

Finally, I never liked receiving either of these two messages: "Is the company being run as if it were public? Or is it the family toy and existing to enable the playful choices of family members?" I liked the gestalt of a public company because of the required discipline in answering to the outside investors. It's professional all the way.

Board of Directors

If you think you need a board of directors, it should be for these reasons:

1. It forces discipline into the organization. (I like people looking over my shoulder.)
2. It moves you in the direction you want to go.
3. It helps you transition the organization into a new generation/management change.
4. It gives the CEO a cushion and advice on tough decisions.
5. It gives support through crisis situations.

We have always found that our best directors were the ones who were currently on, or had, multi-board experience and weren't afraid to challenge us. A wonderful pool of talent to draw from today are the many retired CEOs. If he or she is not retired, be sure a new director is associated with a company that is functioning well and properly.

A director does not have to expound on anything. They just have to ask deep and profound questions. A quiet director is a useless one. Management needs to be challenged by their board. If management takes umbrage when being advised or given comments, then shame on them, as they are headed for the dustbin of history.

It is *very* important that a successful, retiring board *chairman* or founder step *way back*. However, by remaining as a board member, they will be a great backdrop (or insurance) should the new CEO not work out. (And many of them don't!) Too, they need to be a silent and reflective director or it will be a disaster. Their *tribal knowledge* is their forte.

The *most* important duty of a board is CEO selection. And, when selecting, the board must look further into the future than the *current* CEO's vision. That is very difficult for a board and the reason you need sharp and seasoned directors. If succession planning isn't happening, it is the ultimate fault of the board. Unfortunately, most corporate boards spend too much time on oversight (financial) and not enough time on strategy (vision).

Only about 20 percent of private companies have a formal board strong enough to advise on major issues such as a sale, mergers, etc. And, if you have an inside board, you really do not have one at all. I feel the evolution of a board is like this for an entrepreneurial company: It starts as family members only. Then bankers and lawyers are added along the way. The next groups are friends and acquaintances who have been successful, and finally (if a company makes it that far), they begin sculpting the board in a direction they want the company to go. That group should include some multi-board members who have experience with larger companies. Boards and companies should create each other.

This last bit of wisdom. Early on, our CEO Anne Klamar decided to run the company with much more transparency than I ever did. This was a great decision on her part.

To accentuate this, she invited her key managers to sit in the back of our boardroom during meetings (except for brief executive sessions).

Although they did not participate in the dialogue, the managers were able to hear the concerns and advice of different board members. This turned out to be a wonderful method of mentoring as it exposed them to some very strong people and advice. It was a real win:win.

PART FOUR:
BEING FIRST

Leadership

Leadership is the act of believing in something so much that you actually have a *passion* for it, even though you may have to *swim against the tide* to achieve it.

For example, we moved our entire organization to a different town to get away from constant union activity and create room for expansion. We wanted to be appreciated as a resource and a place for career growth. My personal family left where we had been for forty-seven years, knowing that it would be the end of friendships and recognition. It was difficult, but the passion paid off and we became very happy in our new environment, and the organization really took off and blossomed. To uproot was an instinctive decision but, no doubt, the toughest decision my family and I ever made. Midmark actually went from being a sparrow to a swan overnight.

Leadership is actually all about courage. Good leaders want to know bad news or the potential of bad news, immediately, and they are not afraid of the challenge. President Eisenhower said, "Leadership is like pulling a string along (leading by example). If you attempt to push it (leading by force) you will go nowhere."

As a leader, you can be shown a better way to do things without feeling insulted. A good leader can accept good news or bad. The news will be accepted, digested, and appreciated. A non-leader might lose his or her temper because he or she didn't see the problem in the first place.

Leaders are optimistic. Leaders are curious. Leaders are able to anticipate, look ahead, and see around corners. They have vision in spades! They see the big picture.

Leaders are able to persuade people to help in building something larger than they are, as a person. Most people want to be associated with something great, something of which they will be proud—a *touchstone* that puts some magic into an otherwise potentially dull life! A leader provides that vehicle for accomplishment and self-fulfillment.

For twenty years at Midmark, we have had gain sharing for all employees. It has become a team *mantra* and each employee averages approximately $2,000-plus in share gains per year. Furthermore, each month our bulletin boards show the amount versus the cumulative amount of last year's comparison. It is paid out only once a year; around December 1, so that everyone has a great Christmas. Also, we pay this out once a year so that they get a *chunky* amount, chunky enough so they can do something profound with it instead of dribbling small amounts each month or quarter. This is another method we use in trying to make the teammates feel part of the team, and a winning team's results are shown to them each month.

The leader of the future will be a leader of leaders, not a manager of managers.

Leaders are motivators. And if you're successful, Will Rogers will remind you to not take leadership cavalierly: "If you're riding ahead of the herd, take a look back every now and then to make sure it's still there."

A leader's main strength is psychology, versus finance. Selecting the right people to help is paramount. The leader will have the common touch with everyone from a vice president to a janitor. Everyone has to feel comfortable around a real leader. Leaders spend time with their people and listen to them compassionately. With that done, public relations will take care of itself. People are your only sustainable advantage and they come from the selection and retention or (rejection) of a strong leader.

A leader builds self-confidence in others… "I just know you

will handle this project well." The quality of leadership (and thus management) is the single most important asset that determines the prowess or success of any organization. Leadership is what drives results. Leadership is *about* results.

Poor leadership symptoms:	Good leadership ingredients:
Lack of personal accountability	A track record of courage
Fear of making decisions	Vision: getting to the next level
Organizational power struggle	Cultural compatibility and
Re-active vs. proactive	approachability
management	Humility
Committee decisions only	Comes from an organization
	that *has it together*

A strong focus on results will create other leaders. So vision from the leader is very important. Leadership is about taking positions or having ideas that others may think are wrong, and seeing them through to fruition. Leaders aren't afraid of public opinion. They are dogmatic people and don't hesitate to say what is on their mind. They are aware that occasionally they will be caught in the crossfire and this doesn't faze them. Leaders are incredibly ambitious, not for themselves but for the cause and their organization or whatever their objective may be.

Leaders feel okay with themselves. They are extremely confident people and happy in their own skin. (Becoming a leader is all about finding the leader inside oneself.) They don't forget who they are or how they got to where they are. They know their limits and do not forget who *took them to the dance*. They are very aware and active in their community as well. I've seen several cases of owners and managers who think they are too big to mingle with the community. That is a big step towards failure.

Leaders have boundless energy and still have reserve power when others crash. They relish and thrive on change. In fact, leadership is all about managing change. They have the ability to energize others and can get them to move mountains. Leaders constantly test new things and also motivate people around them to do so. They choose and grow strong people.

They can admit mistakes and are able to make decisions rather quickly and execute them, as well. When in a very tight spot, they maintain their integrity and act and decide accordingly. They remain confident in a crisis! A. G. Lafley, chairman of Procter & Gamble, said: "Personal values are not negotiable. They create personal and corporate success." "Leaders aren't born; they are forged in the heat of battle."

Personally, I have always been thankful for tough times. One builds strength by giving out tough assignments where success is in no way guaranteed. To help guarantee success, you surround yourself with strong people and assign mentors who can be rotated in and out every two years. Mentorship should be part of the job description of senior managers.

Fred Smith, CEO of Fed Ex (incidentally, we supplied them with stainless steel drop boxes when we were in the fabricated steel business), said, "The art of leadership is being able to subordinate one's self-interest to the greater good of the organization." Personally, my family knew that Midmark was very high in the list of my priorities. Midmark was an extension of my family!

Good leaders lead without being intrusive, so at the end of the day their people can say, "We did it ourselves!" Leaders know that future leaders learn by example. That is why good leaders produce good leaders. They say what they mean openly and then do what they say. You will be considered a leader when people trust you. Technical skills can be taught much easier than things like trust.

Trust can only be learned over time by example.

Some ingredients I've learned to look for when selecting a leader are:

1. Are they first-born? If so, they have lived leadership.
2. Did they play sports? If so, they know how to compete, learned to trust others, and know the value of team spirit, and thus love to win.
3. Were they an Eagle Scout or equivalent? This tells me about persistence and tenacity.
4. Have they known and conquered adversity?

If a teammate respects a leader, you've got ignition. Respect is the most important of all the leadership qualities. And, at the end of the day, the true and final test of leadership is knowing when to step down. In my case, I was afraid as I got older, I would drag the company down with me.

Finally, this personal note: One day I got a surprise knock on my door. It was a group of teammates carrying a wooden staff with a crook at the top. They presented it to me and explained that they thought I had made a pretty good shepherd. Emotionally, it was my finest moment and I keep it in my office to this day.

Strategy

Over 400 years ago, the legendary Japanese swordsman, Miyamoto Musashi, was quoted as saying, "Perception is strong and sight weak. In strategy it is important to see distant things as if they were close and to take a distanced view of close things."

Where were these words when I needed to hear them forty years ago?

In the late '60s and early '70s, the buzz word was *diversify*. Our company was in construction equipment, foundry equipment, metal fabrications, and medical equipment and with less than $15 million in sales. This was a flawed strategy. We needed to focus for success! Denny Meyer, our executive vice-president, always pushed for diversifying *within* the health-care industry. Today, that is exactly what we are doing, very successfully.

The mistake I made was going into construction equipment, because I thought our medical table market was too small to get to the nine figures I had always wanted. Then, I discovered that the key to success was focus, focus, focus!

Many times investors make the same mistake I did, thinking they'll spread the risk by owning a lot of different companies. In reality, they increase the risk because they are no longer focused. Granted there is risk in over-focusing, too, but at least you'll see the train coming before it rolls over you. Correspondingly, try to make yourself almost impossible to duplicate (like bringing your customers in by corporate jet). Look so awesome to potential competitors that the industry words will be, "Attack anyone except Company A!"

Whatever you do or make, be sure it is hard to duplicate by a competitor or an entrepreneur. This could include distribution quirks and methods. Barriers to entry are wonderful. The *whole* of your strategy should be greater than the sum of the parts.

Connect your dots and focus with a top, winning strategy.

There are riches in niches. The reason our organization has stayed under the big organizations' radar, such as Johnson & Johnson, is that we serve niches too small for their interests. Thus, our combined organization is essentially a collection of relatively small niches joined at the hip. I think of us as a rosary: each business is a decade, and the cross is the sales and marketing (the customer).

Sometimes the strategy doesn't work. Don't be afraid to admit a mistake! Be a big person, admit a mistake early, and move fast to correct it. A mistake's gestation time should be extremely brief.

After my first trip to Europe many years ago, I was impressed by the different countries' lack of size compared to the U.S. I could see tremendous U.S. advantage in the economies of scale. Correspondingly, I returned from Japan in the late '80s and gave a talk to our management, and others, stating, "The U.S. has the wherewithal to beat Japan with one hand tied behind our back." People thought I had *lost it*! My judgment was based on Japan's lack of resources, their population per square mile, and keeping everyone employed in a population of 70 million people.

In relation to the above, I now feel that scale will help, but it will not necessarily make you competitive. Intellectual capital makes you competitive. Leverage your brainpower to success and if you can't, you had better get out. Smart people aren't a commodity, but there are plenty of them. The trick is to keep them teamed and focused.

I have always liked the author Peter Drucker's question, "If you weren't in that business already, would you enter it today?" We subscribe to the theory: if we can't be Number One or Number Two, don't get into that business, and if in it, get out of it. I understand Drucker gave that advice to Jack Welch of General Electric.

A Peter Drucker quote from *Managing in the Next Society:* "With the shrinking world in mind, you cannot survive simply as a manufacturing company unless it is well-niched. You must become a knowledge company based on distribution capabilities. Manufacturing is too easily replicated today. It no longer adds a lot of value. Value is created in knowledge and distribution." Fortunately, Midmark is moving in that direction today. It is our strategy.

What is your strategy when you've made a mistake? Do you have the courage and discipline to get out of things you shouldn't be in? It takes humility to admit a mistake. Always remember, ego has killed more organizations than competition ever will. Construction equipment and hospital products were two large mistakes of mine and we got out of them. I might also add that I have always felt someday we may very well get back into hospital products as there was great synergistic compatibility from an engineering and manufacturing standpoint. The alternate-care market and the hospital markets have been growing closer in recent years. Perhaps someday we will make a large enough acquisition to give us the hospital toehold that we could never create on our own. A major building block of strategy is deciding what *not* to do!

Here is one thing not to do: Never attack a privately held, solidly positioned company that has a strong balance sheet and relatively young management. You'll get creamed because they remember distinctly the money they had to borrow and the struggle to get their vision accomplished. Instead, attack an old public company that is deeply in debt. Their leadership is generally weak, and their underbellies are soft. They also have to present their financial status to their outside investors every ninety days to keep their stock price up.

In 1999 we sold off our hospital equipment group and moved our Asheville, North Carolina, dental plant into our highly efficient hallmark Versailles operation. It absolutely destroyed our profit and loss that year, but our balance sheet held, and it proved to be two brilliant moves simultaneously. Our vice president of manufacturing, Karl Weidner, and our plant manager in Asheville, Mike Walker, did an impeccable planning job in execution of the above.

And to prove that we still believe in the theory: "If we're not having fun, we're doing it wrong," our vice president of finance, Rich Bunce (who came to us with international experience by way of G.E./Gillette) handled the divestiture. I told Rich that if he could get us out of the hospital market *whole,* I would push him to the county seat in a wheelbarrow. He delivered and I didn't, but we do have a hallmark photo of me pushing him, somewhere, in a wheelbarrow.

Strategically, we did not feel our franchise in the hospital market was strong enough. The hospital market did not look that robust to us, and it was a process-sell instead of a dealer-sell which we understood. Plus, we had the template to take that skill set into the dental and veterinarian market. We were right! But if your best people haven't been included in setting your current strategy and, thus, do not have a definite buy-in, it is not going to work properly.

Constantly put your competition under a microscope and study their every move. *Your* strategy depends on this. Many times you can build a good business by working the small niches they are not interested in.

Never, ever, underestimate competition, especially new competition. We proved this at market entry thirty years ago and have held our position ever since. Never forget what the Japanese did to Detroit while Detroit laughed about the rice burners. This is a good example of what was once a seemingly invincible position. And to think that I used to watch semis on our nearest interstate I-75 that stated, *Cadillac: Standard of the World!*

We recently had a new attacker in our base product offering. It was the best thing that could have happened to us. Due to an extended high market share position, we were falling asleep. Thank you competition!

Only do what you do best! Let the suppliers do what they do best. That will enable you to do well in what you do and focus,

focus, focus. One of the reasons small organizations stay small is they try to do and make anything the customer wants or asks. No strategy!

Changing the rules has built many great businesses. An extremely interesting business model was Trader Joe's. Instead of thinking *sell groceries*, they concentrated on *buying food*. From the start they sent their buyers worldwide and sought out unusual and high value items that were a niche relatively overlooked by competition. What a success story!

Always remember, nothing is forever. So strategize for the future.

A good written strategy should fit on one page.

At the very heart of every good strategy is deep, deep understanding of the customer (or market, which are the same). I cannot emphasize that enough.

One way to understand your customer is to slice and dice your markets to discover underserved niches. As I have said before, there are riches in niches. It is better to be a large part of a small market than a small part of a large market. You can really learn to understand the customer niche.

Work at or create a business that is hard to duplicate. Personally, I have never felt commodity markets interesting or challenging. Establish a difference you can preserve.

Work toward fewer moving parts. I have never seen a *complex* strategy succeed yet! Focus. Become customer concentric, and move when they do, or you will be left in the dustbin of time.

If you are making a major strategy change, make sure your company culture can and does change to accommodate the new direction as we did in entering the medical field and leaving a manufacturing strategy for a marketing one.

In strategy, denial is probably the biggest impediment to survival. Being honest with one's self does not come easily. But it is most important for survival. In one company where I was on the board, I saw their business slipping in spite of running an efficient organization. There was a paradigm market shift that I felt was very obvious. Their market segment had shifted away from them, but they could not see that. Their response was to work harder and change tactical effort. Nothing worked because they were getting their only feedback from distributors that were stuck in the same trough. At least 20 percent of the total market had shifted, but they refused to acknowledge it. The tinkering they did to try to fix it only added more confusion to the confusion that was already there. Listen to the customers. They are the market. They will help you focus on the new strategy.

You will *always* find your answer with your customer. Besides, they keep you in business. The distributor does not have your answer; the customer has it and will always have it. Your insight must come from outside the organization.

Finally, connect the dots, as described above, to create your business model. In each enterprise there is a profit *sweet spot*. In your business model that is your *peg* (or core competency). Strategically, work out from that point. I have been on corporate boards and could easily spot the *sweet spot* and yet watch the management continually work further and further away from their *peg*, to eventually get into trouble. Your entire market is your target, but your main profit engine has to be the bull's eye.

Procter & Gamble bought a friend of mine's pet food organization (Iams) at a strong figure. I asked P&G chairman A.G. Lafley what precipitated that decision. "One of our three main thrusts is nutrition. Most pet food companies are outgrowths or by-products of the grain industry. The organization we bought was based on nutrition and not grain. That was the catalyst."

He saw that distant thing and made it close. Good vision. Great strategy.

Taglines

We have always believed in, and used, taglines. Taglines and organizations (people) should essentially create each other.

Our first was penned by our advertising firm and associate, Bob Oppenheim. We have used it for over thirty years and it is timeless and flexible. *BECAUSE WE CARE* is a tagline of only three words, but today they are highly valuable. It acts as a guidepost for us as we move forward.

We have several others, but they're not officially stated, such as, *"Easy to buy from,"* which has helped us. *"Look to Midmark for the answer,"* is a good driver for us. Another one that acts as an anchor is, *"Everything is negotiable but our integrity!"* Finally, my favorite, *"If we're not having fun, we are doing it wrong."*

Mr. Oppenheim also penned the slogan for the village where we are headquartered. *"People, Pride, Progress"* has served the village well and is timeless. It has acted as a driver because Versailles, Ohio, has just continually gotten better!

A competitor of a company where I was a board member used, *"First, because we last."*

Quite clever, I thought.

Tenacity

Our high school recently had to switch leagues. We had a strong legacy, especially in football, winning multiple state championships in our original league. In reality, our kids, both boys and girls, excelled in all sports. The new league put us in competition with much bigger kids and I thought, "There goes that legacy!"

Well, within three years, we not only beat every team in that league, we went on to again win the state championship. We rose to the occasion, which again proves that competition is good for you. Quitting is not an option. Quitting something means that you don't have the *guts* to correct what the problem was in the first place. To me it means that you might quit at the next hurdle, too. It would have been easier not to quit the steel fabrication business and not go into the medical field. That transition took about ten frustrating years, but they were fun years, too, as we were achieving new goals and we could actually see our progress as we moved the *DNA* of the company.

From cancer survivor and Tour De France winner, Lance Armstrong: "Pain is temporary, quitting lasts forever."

One of our favorite sayings is, "We might be wrong, but we are never uncertain." I always feel that persons with convictions are masters of those who doubt.

Finally, this comment from Herb Kelleher, founder of Southwest Airlines, and known for his cigarettes and Wild Turkey. When asked why he never quit smoking, he quipped, "My mom taught me to never be a quitter, and I don't want to disappoint her."

Well, there *are* exceptions…

Timing is Everything

At the turn of the 18th century and even later, fifty-year store leases were not uncommon if they were located on trolley lines. Phone booths seemed to be a recession-proof business. Little yellow film boxes were seemingly eternal. The time was right for that method, that service, and that product.

But there is never a wrong time to make the right change.

Our move into the medical field was deliberate and couldn't have been timed better. The time to *buy in* to any situation is before its potential is seen by others. Our new Midmark president's move into the vet market is a classic example of this. In terms of positioning, *"The best way to get where you are going is to be where you are."*

Peter Drucker advises, "To do five years later what it would have been smart to do five years earlier is a sure recipe for frustration or failure."

So, when you go to a cocktail party and everyone is discussing the incredible prices of homes, it is time to buy stocks, and vice versa. In California, since the sub-prime lending fiasco, much of the cocktail conversation is about the prices of real estate. In addition to high prices, there are some huge savings in value in southern California. Too, people love to talk about their homes, as they are usually their greatest assets and possibly have been very profitable for them.

But, before you break out the champagne, do the math. Unless you bought in a real estate value trough, you may be *underwater* when you consider all your costs. (Rent is really cheap if prices have spiked!)

Bottom line? Your selling price of something very dear to you can vary drastically depending upon whether you do or do not *have to sell* it. Thus, timing is everything.

PART FIVE: THE SKILL SET

Management

Leadership is vision, whereas management is making the right things happen at the right time and in the right way.

I was on a panel in the '70s at the University of Dayton with Jim McSwinny, chairman of Mead Corporation. I commented that I had to go to Cincinnati and join the Society for Advancement of Management (SAM) to find out about management. A brilliant man, he quipped, "What *is* it?" We subsequently started our own chapter of SAM and, following that, I started Midmark University, a two-and-one-half-day seminar to train our people, internally, on management. This was our first step in unlocking our people's potential. It was there all the time. The *doors* just needed to be *opened*.

Here are some things I learned at UD and our associates learned at Midmark University:

Management meetings should be full of robust disagreement if you want a strong, objective organization or company.

Someone who isn't *getting it* needs to be told to improve immediately and repeatedly. Then, if they don't step up to the plate, there will be no surprises when they are dismissed. Of course, if the cards are played right, they will leave on their own and exit without a lot of embarrassment or loss of face. If a person is not performing, it is a sign that they'll probably perform better somewhere else. Give them the respect of allowing them to do that and move quickly. You never pull a band-aid off slowly.

If a new teammate hired into a key position hasn't made some profound changes in their area in six months, you had better be concerned. At twelve months, they should be gone.

Where does job security come from? To start with, any organization that puts job security first is headed for the dustbin of history. Job security comes from listening and doing what your customer and markets want. As a general comment, the people who expect job security are generally not strong enough to create it.

If, as a manager, you have trouble saying, "No," don't expect to be around too long!

Second tier management should operationally run the organization. Your top people are there to grow it. A manager needs to be both tough and inspirational! And, if you are not expecting big things to happen by being tough, you are not fair to your people and ultimately yourself.

And finally, if a manager has more than three to four goals, either they, their boss, or both, are foolish.

Listening & Communication

It seems that the subject of listening and communicating has been on human minds for at least 5000 years. If not, why are there so many references to it in the Jewish faith (and Buddhism and Islam, as well)?

"Better eloquent silence than eloquent speech." "When a fool holds his tongue, he, too, is thought clever." "A wise man hears one word and understands two." These are three Jewish proverbs from which we can learn about listening and communication.

Whether it's with your teammates, customers, or family, listening is, without a doubt, the most important ingredient for success. It ultimately solves everything if you have the empathy that needs to go with it. Listen devoutly! And if the answer to your question is evasive—get nervous. Someone is likely trying to hide something. ("Better eloquent silence than eloquent speech.")

Without a doubt, the people on your plant floors know the areas, equipment, and work flow. They know how things are run. They are the best. Smart people listen to them. You see, people in high places have 20 percent of the information but make 80 percent of the decisions. ("A wise man hears one word and understands two.")

We once hired a high-level executive into our organization. He thought more highly of himself than anyone else thought of him. His ego overshadowed every conversation and his mind was so focused on himself and what he was about that he heard nothing or very little from anyone else. That same ego went right to our customers and their needs, and our new product offerings dwindled down to nothing. His ego killed him and he was eventually asked to leave. ("When a fool holds his tongue, he, too, is thought clever," couldn't have helped this fellow.)

We have consistently found that the smartest people are the best listeners. The longer they wait to respond, the better and more intelligent are their responses. Train yourself to be such a good listener that the person you are conversing with feels like he or she is the only person in the room. (This gem from Will Rogers: "Never miss a good chance to shut up.")

When communicating, first and foremost, be honest. Tell it like it is. No sugar coating please—it is very unfair to the receiver. If you, as a manager, are not honest, the people who work for you will suffer and your company will, as well. Besides, it is impossible to tell only one lie—you have to keep lying to cover your tracks.

People and organizations that survive and thrive have honest, linked relationships—not processes. It is people, people, people!

To make a message clear, think it through carefully before you speak. You want the receiver of your message to hear what you mean to convey. State the message in a way that convinces the people of your intention.

Always, always, always be thoughtful. Think of the other person first. If you can train yourself to do that, you will be very successful in anything you do. When communicating on the phone, let your *smile* be heard.

Don't be afraid to ask the *dumb* questions. You will motivate a lot of smart people who will understand you're interested in knowing answers. The only dumb question is the one that wasn't asked.

After too many union elections and knowing how self-serving unions have become, we decided our problem was communication. Thus, in addition to newsletters and bulletins, we initiated quarterly town hall meetings where we spoke to the entire organization. The subjects were business opportunities, competition, equipment purchases, and other relevant newsworthy items. These meetings gave everyone a chance to contribute and feel that they were an important part of the organization. This served the purpose better than unionizing.

A smart director once told me that you can do almost anything, as long as you tell your employees first. This includes accurately sharing all your financial data. If you're not, you are not being fair to yourself or your people. Your people need fresh numbers to make them believe in you and the company. You can't manage a secret.

And just in case this all makes sense to you, read this famous quote from Alan Greenspan, former chairman of the U.S. Federal Reserve, in addressing a congressional committee: "I guess I should warn you, if what I say turns out to be particularly clear, you've probably misunderstood what I've said."

Delegation

A CEO manages the results. He or she hires and appoints the right people to create the results that will fulfill the vision to be achieved. That is delegation.

As you grow, eventually you will not be able to make all the decisions. You will have to delegate to people you feel you can trust to help in making decisions. Many times they will make decisions that are ugly and you, as a leader, get caught in the cross-fire and are blamed. If you can't accept the fate of taking blame for something you didn't do, you cannot be a leader.

Delegation can be an ego thing. It has to do with being a secure person. If you allow yourself to believe that someone might be as smart, or smarter, than you, and you give them the authority to do a job without interference, then you're a manager and a leader.

When someone spends their time doing things that people below them can do as well, they are a wasted asset and prevent themselves and others from growing. The problem is not with the employee, it is with the boss not being able to give up power.

Be willing to accept less-than-perfect for awhile as the employee learns. Be willing to allow mistakes and keep your mouth shut as the employee takes on more responsibility.

When you delegate, don't criticize the person if what he or she does isn't perfect. Instead, criticize the event or situation tactfully, not the person.

Problem? Do nothing and see who shows up to fix it. Then let them. That's how you spot your strong, creative people.

Out of town? Tell employees what you want done and when. Then, don't call in. Let them stand on their own two feet.

Look at the caliber of people behind a boss, and I'll tell you quickly how good of a delegator/leader they are.

Finally, looking at major corporations like G.E., Emerson Electric, etc., and other large organizations, you can see that they are built on de-centralization. The top people know how to delegate and to whom to delegate.

Discipline

Every manager/director should read *Good to Great*, written by Jim Collins. He has this to say: "When you have people who are disciplined, you don't need hierarchy; when you have disciplined thought, you don't need bureaucracy; when you have disciplined action, you don't need excessive controls. When you get a combination of discipline with an ethic of entrepreneurship, you get the magical alchemy of great performance."

Fred Smith, CEO of Fed Ex, says, "Anyone who works themselves into exhaustion or incoherence doesn't have the discipline to lead the organization to begin with." In many ways, the disciplined organization has ended up being that way as a result of adversity. Adversity is good; it gives us *spin and spine*. It gives us the strength to move forward, to correspond and further discipline ourselves and the organization.

"Eat your own cooking" is a favorite phrase of Warren Buffett. I interpret it as meaning that you should live with what you've created. Spend time with product users, dealers, employees, suppliers, community and shareholders. Personally, I love to hear complaints, as they are responsible for progress and they keep us from getting complacent. Ask, "What is your biggest problem?" And then listen devoutly. There is no substitute for spending time in the field.

The reason so many vision statements end up in the dustbin of time is the organization's leadership doesn't have the discipline to refer to them frequently and to follow them diligently.

Goals

You must have goals. Actually, they are fun to reach, but the real fun is in working towards them. It's not how many goals you have, but the quality of the goals you're trying to attain.

After college, I found a 1935 Ford rumble seat convertible sitting in a field about fifty miles from home. I bought it for $75. It was sitting in the mud, the top was gone, and it even had bees in the seat. Including a stint in the army, it took me six years to get it totally restored. I sold it a year or two after fixing it up and moved on to sports cars. It was simply no longer fun. I always found the same thing with model airplanes. Once completed, the fun is over!

In an organization, I feel three to four annual goals are enough. Some of these spill over into other mini goals. Goals must be set by top management, as their leadership should contain the vision. The goals need to be long term toward a *constantly* articulated vision. The greatest impediment to the above is short-term focus. And knee-jerk cost cutting will slow you considerably.

Your vision—those long-term goals—should stretch to twenty-five years. I like goals that take decades to finish. Relative to that, once we attained nine figures, I was fulfilled. Not relative to that is the goal of finishing this book, for which I keep looking for new experiences to make it richer. Once it's complete, though, the fun will be over and a new goal will have to be set.

Growth

According to Procter & Gamble, "Organic growth is the most valuable because it comes from your core competency. It is more profitable and valuable because it adds to your inner strength or soul." Growth is opportunity and talent likes to go where opportunity exists.

Everyone can grow. Running out of talent or cash is the limiting factor. One of my favorite sayings is, "The cream always goes to the bottom...and it is called cash!" You cannot grow yourself out of trouble.

We have had years when we grew the top line 40 percent and the bottom along with it. However, we could not sustain it, as no one has that much talent or capital. We like to think an average of 10 percent growth is a good number. Even 20 percent growth is probably not sustainable, but it has been done.

If you are anticipating strategic moves, such as moving into new markets, you had better have a core business that is operating smoothly. When acquiring a new company, you can spread your talent too thin, and drain your cash until it is up and running. The easiest and most focused, risk-free way to grow is by getting closer to existing customers and striving to serve them better. They will love you for it!

Hiring

Hiring is the least scientific and most risky thing management personnel must do.

A prospective employee who interviews well, might merely indicate that he or she is good at interviewing...and may have done it often.

When hiring a high-level person, *always* have that person take a professional psychological (personality) test. It can save not only cash, but heartaches, as well.

Personally, if I have a choice between someone who's very bright and someone who's very gutsy, I'll take the gutsy person, anytime. Smart people are everywhere, courageous ones are rare.

I always like the idea of throwing out some bait and seeing who shows up. Walter Wriston of Citicorp said, "If you've got the wrong people in the wrong spots there is nothing you can do to save the situation. If you've got the right ones in the right spots, there is nothing you can do to screw it up!" Those people are your safety nets!

From Herb Kelleher of Southwest Airlines, "We hire attitudes. You can coach and train skills, but attitudes are hard to create." The hardest thing for your competition to imitate is attitude. Look for courage, humility, selflessness, and altruism.

As an organization, know and never forget who you are. Midmark has become a somewhat deep-cultured and storied corporation. Hiring those who fit our culture is not easy, but we have proven over the years it can be done, wisely.

Mentors

Ask any successful person how he or she became successful and that person probably will tell you of at least one strong mentor in their lives. I was very fortunate and had many good mentors, although I do think *I* was able to spot *them*.

If your organization doesn't have an assigned mentor program, establish one now. And, don't forget the chemistry. If it's not there, it's a waste of time. The mentors should choose who they want to work with in order for it to be most successful. It will pay off big time. G.E. and Toyota have a wonderful mentoring program. Managers are judged on how well they lead and nurture their people.

If you are a mentor, you must give good feedback along the way in order to be effective. Feedback gives reassurance that your *student* is on the right track. One time, I was asked to mentor a young manager from another state. Since our time together was limited, I prepared and presented this list to him:

- Make a profit and watch your balance sheet daily.
- Grow the business.
    You cannot build a company by yourself. You can only build an organization and the organization builds the business.
- Keep focused, but have some fun, too.
    Time in the field is extremely important. Don't be deluded into thinking that you're too busy at the office to travel. Your market is not at the office. It is everywhere.
- Love your people and you will gain their respect in return.
    Work harder than anyone else and make people aware of it, not in talking about it but allowing them to observe it.
- Learn to read your people so that you can trust them.
- The purpose of any business is to serve the customer.
- Read the *Wall Street Journal, Forbes, Fortune* and *Business Week*.
    Think big, but develop a reputation for really being frugal on everything except service to the customer. Dimes truly do make dollars.
- Move quickly.

- Work with a minimum of paperwork and always remember that what gets measured, gets done. All items should have a rigid timeline.
- Set limits. It is the leader's job!
  Steve Covey said, "There's more control in a system of trust than in a system of controls."
- Be honest. Tell it like it is and never duck an issue.
- Be humble. Don't let success go to your head.
- Promote the people who challenge you. They will be the decision makers.
- Always do your toughest job first.
- Give more than you get. It always comes back to you.
- Look for opportunities to mentor.

Finally this: I was being mentored without realizing it, thinking the mentor was just being kind to me. I was sad when he *pushed the boat out* and let me paddle alone. It was time for me to make my own decisions. To this day, I am so grateful.

Mistakes

Failure will be your best friend if you'll let it. It is without a doubt the greatest learning tool there is. Here again, honesty comes into play. If you cannot recognize and admit mistakes quickly, you are sentencing yourself to a lifetime of failures. Being in denial is not being honest.

When mistakes are made it is not time for criticizing; it is a great time for encouragement and confidence building. The ability to spot and quickly admit a mistake is priceless indeed. It separates success from failure, as success is simply a series of corrected errors. Mistakes are like the tacks of a sailboat. The tacks are directional decision points and error corrections. And the sooner an error is corrected, the sooner you will reach your destination.

If you want to be recognized as a leader, the people who follow you must hear you admit your mistakes, explain what you did wrong, hear how you'll avoid it in the future, and welcome your request for their advice.

I believe most big mistakes come from a lack of planning and a lack of honesty with oneself (living in denial). Most are made not out of ignorance but simply from a lack of information. Mistakes are a bi-product of haste. Tom Watson of IBM has this to say about mistakes: "To succeed, double your failure rate!"

The founder of Honda insisted on originality and innovation. He said, "Success is ninety-nine percent failure."

My approach has always been to lead from behind. Give others the credit and you take the blame for the mistake. As president, every mistake ultimately rests at your feet. This takes the immediate heat off the person making the mistake, although the person making the mistake knows the truth.

One of our favorite sayings is: "We might be wrong, but we're never uncertain!"

If we had to list all of our mistakes, they would fill a second book twice the size of this one.

Motivation

What is motivation? I believe it is leadership in disguise.

One of our first big motivational acts was giving our key people a chance to buy a tiny amount of stock financed by the organization. It was no giveaway. They had to pay for it at a modest interest rate. No one was pressured and everyone who was asked, subscribed.

In 1970, when we won the American Iron & Steel Institute Award for the design of our first product, the presentation was at the Waldorf Astoria in New York City. I asked Dave Bester, our project leader, and John Oldiges, our engineer, to represent us and receive the award. These were two great, humble guys. This honor gave them pride in themselves and the company. I was purposely not there.

Over the years, Esther and I attended many worldwide meetings of the Young Presidents Organization (YPO). We brought home to our managers aquamarines from Brazil, Pigeon Eye rubies from Thailand...gemstones from wherever we had been. I could buy good quality at an attractive price, and there is no duty on bringing cut stones into the U.S. We rewarded people with management parties—first in our home, thanks to Esther. Eventually, when we were able to afford our local country club, our events were held there.

When we hit $5 million and $10 million in sales, our people and our advertising and design firms were each given a $5 and a $10 gold piece to commemorate reaching those goals. I suppose the highest impact event was when we hit $50 million in sales. We had a dinner at the country club and each officer/manager was given fifty shares of the company stock. I remember Esther giving out the envelopes (having just personally moved to our new home and plant location) and I was stating that the contents of that envelope, when looking ahead, would be worth far more than the value of our home. My comments were prophetic!

Being grateful, expressing appreciation, and rewarding employees' hard work, are thoughtful ways to motivate them for the future. Although you cannot push someone up a ladder, I always liked to sneak an idea into their head. If that someone takes ownership of that idea, they then feel it is *their* idea, and there is no holding them back. Showing thanks can be an *idea*. It's the idea that loyalty and hard work are rewarded. And it's a great motivator.

Even though most people have their own agenda, and many times it's financially-based (everyone has to eat and pay their bills), I think these four items by author and speaker, Jan Carlzon, speak towards motivation:

1. Everyone needs to know and feel that they are needed.
2. Everyone wants to be treated as an individual.
3. Giving someone the freedom to take responsibility releases resources that would otherwise remain concealed.
4. An individual without information cannot take responsibility; an individual who is given information cannot help but take responsibility.

These are the words of a motivator, a leader in disguise.

Team Building

Randy Gump, the city manager of our village, liked to say, "Surround yourself with good people and wonderful things will happen." And he has a track record to prove that to be true.

From *Good to Great* by Jim Collins, "The people in great companies loved what they did largely because they loved who they were doing it with." The best relationships result when both parties need each other! People and organizations tend to create each other. I find the same to be true with boards of directors.

The managers who are not developing must leave.

Correspondingly, you are not doing an employee a favor by retaining them if they are incompetent. Why? They'll do a better job working at something that truly suits them. You aren't being kind to someone by retaining them until they are 55, and then getting them caught in a people cutback. However, if someone is merely acceptable, is dedicated, a team player, accepted by his or her co-workers, and a hard worker, you simply move them to where they will be more competent. You need people like that in the organization too.

Never forget, being nice just to be nice, can be an unkindness. If someone isn't *cutting it,* be honest. At six-month intervals, they must be told, honestly. Perhaps people around them are getting raises while they are not. At that point, they'll have enough sense to begin looking outside the organization for a new position and you, as their boss, should do your best to help them reposition themselves somewhere else. Again, be kind, but truthful.

Tough Decisions

Approximately thirty years ago, National Cash Register Corporation (NCR), in Dayton, Ohio, was an organization that focused on mechanical products. To bring it up to the digital age, they brought in (from Hong Kong) one of their top people, Bill Anderson. He was brilliant and had to be extremely tough. NCR not only knocked down all their buildings, but ended up laying-off approximately 20,000 people.

In an interview published in the local Dayton paper one Sunday, he was asked how he could do that to all those people. He answered, "I knew I had to hurt some of the people or in the final analysis, I would have hurt them all." Working toward the *greater good* of an organization is paramount.

I remember being called out of retirement. Not only were most of my good people gone, but our costs were out of control. Eliminating company cars and going to co-pay for medical benefits, etc., was not fun, nor did it make me very popular. But I knew if I cared about our people, and I did, tough decisions must be made.

During that same time period, we moved our dental group operation from North Carolina to Versailles and divested our hospital division, resulting in some layoffs, which were rare for us. It proved to be, strategically, the right decision, and it really helped our workforce rather than hurt it. Again, *Focus for Success!*

It took long-term thinking to make these decisions, and they were overdue to be made. I have always found that the sooner you confront issues, the more options you have. Waiting only narrows the options and results in panic and hasty decisions.

From an article by Jim Collins in *Fortune Magazine:* "Companies fail because of what they do to themselves rather than what the world does to them!"

PART SIX:
THE ESSENTIALS

Marketing

The best products are those that the consumers don't know they want. In this digital age, for instance, who knew they might now need or want a GPS. My friend, Heinz Prector, now deceased, came from Germany to the U.S. as a toolmaker and started the American Sun Roof Company (a billion dollar company). He told me, "I spent the first ten years convincing people that cutting a hole in the roof was a good idea." And there was Iacocca's Mustang and minivan. They were built towards a lifestyle. You can't go wrong if you keep researching what the market thinks it needs or even doesn't know it needs.

Thanks to designer Terry Simpkins of Richardson-Smith, we convinced the medical industry that medical equipment should not look clinical, as it did, but have a comfortable furniture look to further soothe the anxiety of the patient. The whole industry eventually converted and we won the American Iron & Steel Institute Award the year that we launched our product. Greatness can begin by being different.

The leader of the future needs to be on top of what the market needs. They must spend time in the marketplace, understand the product and most important, talk to users of products or services so that he or she can get the feel of what they might need. You *don't* get good product ideas internally. They come from the minds of the consumer of your product, and they are not in your office.

We happen to own a small hotel and a conference center. Every year I would make a surprise overnight stay, just to see and feel what our customers felt. Never forget that your future success lies with the customer. They have the answer to your future as no one else does. Listen to them. Important, too, is watching distribution patterns, as they are constantly changing. And you can't do these things by delegation. There are no excuses for the leadership of your organization not to spend lots of time in the marketplace. They will see trends and preferences emerge. They will read between the lines. When talking with customers, the negative answers your organization hears are the platinum ones. It will tell your organization where to go next and you, as leader, how to guide the ship. Listening to the customer is a precious rite.

If your market share is very high, don't overreact and jump into a completely new field as I once did. Make the pond (market) larger by conceiving products that do more for the consumer and for which you can charge more. A good example of this is our taking a non-power-table market and converting it to power. What we initially thought was a $10 million market turned into a $50 million-plus market.

In terms of market share, the cheapest time to build it is when the economy is down. That's when to increase your advertising, trade show efforts, and product development. It is especially fun when your competition is a public company. You can whack their chops if they have earnings pressure because they always have to answer to outside investors. They may be having to cut costs on all *their* marketing efforts.

Slice and dice your marketing data to gain new market insights and open up segmented markets. This can build your overall market. This is called *customer segmentation.*

We recently had a customer come to us with a problem that no one in the market had solved, including us. By working with this customer on a solution, we realized that the product which was evolving and which we were now co-developing, would make our current product obsolete. Knowing that many organizations had destroyed themselves by just hanging on to their successful legacies, we had our new product *take over* the old one (as good as it was). Don't let past history destroy your future by holding on to it.

If you want a future, you had better create one. Working with your organization should be an experience, not an end result. Furthermore, to beat competition, you need to create markets, not just serve them. This is where our new medical doctor-president came in. It was her seminal thought process that proposed "efficient office design" before the equipment itself.

Therefore, we again came out with a new concept that the market did not know it needed but embraced immediately. And we, by listening, *shot the lights out* in our market competition. Too, when she joined the company, we morphed from a metals company making medical products to a true medical equipment company, because *she* understood the consumer and the science of our future products. In the end, the value and price of a product will come from the benefits it brings to the customer.

Today, even though we hear that the world has become *flat,* most people miss the point when it comes to an overseas market. They think of the foreign countries only as a source of cheap product and labor. It is a good idea to own an organization over there, perhaps for the above, but more important, for the marketing opportunities. Think of the millions of people in the Asian countries and the market that they represent. The key is to be there and learn to think as they do. In the U.S., our company designs are created for the top of the market. But in Asia, most people are not going to be wealthy for a long time, but their market is huge if we can design and build for simplicity. Chindia (stands for China and India) must be one of the major cornerstones of any company marketing into the next century.

Good marketing helps the customer to learn to believe. We think a good example is G.M. I am sure they would like me to buy a Buick. But my idea or belief about Buick makes me think of my father's gray hair. I don't want to put myself in that category because I don't feel old. And even though I have gray hair, I'm not particularly crazy about being thought of that way. So, for them to get me to buy, they must market to my alter ego (win some races, new crisp designs, etc.). That takes a long time. At trade shows, Midmark always tries to look twice as big as they are. That is where the seminal beliefs of our customers begin.

Finally, remember it is much, much easier to get into a growing market than a retreating one. In a retreating one, due to less overall market size, every competitor is scrambling to find uncovered niches. In a growing market, you can latch onto an overlooked niche, get a toehold, and *climb*.

Sales

There are three major things to remember about selling:
1. Nothing sells a product like the product that has *already* sold well;
2. Make your product easily accessible for purchase;
3. Make servicing your product quick and pleasant.

Then there are the more subtle, but very important rules: Years ago, in the fabricated steel business, we had a customer who only gave us the tough jobs. The easy jobs went to a supplier with lower overhead because he didn't have the technical staff that we did. Then, due to a mix in their products, we were needed less. Yet, the more our business ebbed with them, the friendlier we got. We don't believe in burning bridges. You never know what the future holds.

Years later, we were a large customer to an organization with whom we had a twenty-five-year relationship. At one of their social functions, Esther and I were more or less snubbed. Their people were too busy talking among themselves. I felt the relationship was taken for granted and their hunger for business had disappeared. We subsequently decided to change suppliers.

Many months later, I saw their president at another social function and I was *really* snubbed! It was obvious that the organization was no longer hungry. I felt they would lose ground because of this. Time proved me right. Today they are only a husk of their former self.

When I was first coaxed out of retirement by our board of directors, I found much in disarray. For one thing, our sales people were considering private labeling our products with our distributors. They didn't realize that we would be giving up some control of our company to distribution. It would be a major step towards going out of business. I railed *against* this and prevailed, and to this day we do no private labeling.

Build your organization or product name into a household word. Make it revered and represent the ultimate in integrity. That name will be your ticket to growth and independence. Should you make the terrible mistake of private labeling (unless it is a small strategic move), you have given away the control of your organization. It is important to run the organization according to *your* own agenda, allowing you to maintain strategic growth. Work toward a broad and integrated line of equipment that your distributors can cherish. A name is a promise, and that name should represent the ultimate in integrity.

When we first started in the medical field, our group manager, Dave Bester, made a wonderful choice of an advertising firm, of which Bob Oppenheim was president. He was just great! We would grouse to him about sales being slow in spite of our advertising. He would then ask, "Have you been out making calls?" The answer was no, and he would then let us have it. "Well, get your butts out there!" We needed that! Customers do not come to you. You've got to go to them. Work on building mind-share, associating a product with a specific company. That is where market share comes from. We always worked on the thesis of relationship-selling with our distributors, who are, for Midmark, our customers. (Midmark doesn't sell products directly to the end-user consumer.) We learned that in the process of selling, if you suddenly feel you need to *build* the relationship with the customer, it's too late. Your competitor already occupies that slot.

Even though your easiest sales are to customers with whom you are already working, keep looking to build more customers because, due to volume increases, your returns will be higher and you can even afford to do some "price shaving" if need be.

I'd like to conclude this section with what we do for our distributors. We are very committed to distributor selling. We are headquartered in a very small town, and when we have people from a key distributor (a major customer) come here, we try to make them never forget where they have been. For example, we may have them falsely arrested, or there may be a plane pulling a banner with their name on it, or they may get a ride on a fire truck, or the high school band might be waiting at the plane when they land. People won't remember a ballgame, golf, or a symphony, but they never forget Versailles, Ohio!

When we make a West Coast sales run in our plane, it ties up our equipment and people for a week. Then we came up with the great idea of placing a showroom in Long Beach, California. We felt it would be effective, and our West Coast company people would love it. Guess what? They turned it down because they felt they would miss the *Versailles Experience*.

Finally, this wise and important comment by entrepreneur/ friend Frank Magid: "No one takes your business away. You *give* it away."

Trade Shows

We are in about 150 shows a year, worldwide. My conclusion is that they are not just about showing your product, they are about making contacts and transferring knowledge. In our second year in the medical field, we didn't have the money to show at the annual trade show in Las Vegas. When we didn't show, guess what our competition said? "Midmark isn't making it. They must be in trouble." So *always* be there, if for no other reason than to keep visible and defend yourself.

Don't just talk about sales—be sales! Don't just make cameo appearances at your trade shows. Work the booth but also make territory calls with your sales people. The answer to your success lies with your customer.

Early on, we would park our one semi-trailer in a highly visible space between the airport and the show so we would be the first and last company seen by potential customers. We also wanted to show we were big enough to *have* a semi-trailer...although our tractor was *used*.

Always give the impression that you are twice as big as you are, and look very professional in all respects. Never forget, *in the mind's eye, perception is reality.*

Value

What is value anyway? It has nothing to do with price alone — especially a cheap price. It is a combination of quality, service, and price. You can't sell value. It is a perceived emotion that belongs to the purchaser. It comes from the benefits the customers think it will bring them.

Value has everything to do with a consumer feeling good, months after their purchase. It helps to have the consumer feel that their buy was better or at least equal to their friends' purchase. Reassurance by others really helps, so communicate and re-communicate a satisfied customer's feedback. Use customer testimonials in your advertising!

In Midmark's case, value is this: Our products are presented to a customer from a distributor who has a very good feeling about this supplier (Midmark) and know that they are a very high integrity company who backs everything with excellent service and warranties. If in doubt, a phone call to our many customers world-wide will prove to them that we are a nearly 100-year-old market share leader. That is what value is all about.

Competition

We once decided to enter a new market dominated by a 50-percent-plus market share player. This is the type of competition we've always tried to avoid, as they are usually private, well-financed, profitable, respected, and well-managed. They have held a long-time solid niche. People like this remember the large amount of debt they had to pay off and how frugal they had to be to pay it off, to reach this point of success. Their people really have exceptional pride.

Initially, we said we wouldn't bother this player as they will be too tough. We'll go after the other smaller players holding market shares from single digits to low double digits.

As we waded into the vortex of that market, we found we naturally ended up competing with the 50-percent-plus player because we found ourselves strong enough to do it. It ended up making us, them, and all the market players, better. We were lucky that time. But my advice is to stay away from a situation like this as 50-percent-plus players can be killers. They remember where they were in earlier years.

Correspondingly, we had a very strong position in another market and got pretty complacent about it until *we* were attacked by a new player. It was the best thing that could have happened to us because it got us energized and we actually enjoyed the challenge.

Benchmarking, or copying, will eventually only get you to where the company you are copying was three to five years before. Meanwhile, they have moved on. The market leader's features do not come from software or equipment, they come from their intellectual capital, which is impossible to copy, and their deep understanding and attention to the market.

The reason to be very cautious in deciding to compete with an entrepreneurial company that is still run by its founder is that you'll have to be as adaptable as they are to compete with them. Never forget, the adaptability genes are still in that organization, versus very old, successful organizations that wouldn't consider changing anything because they have been so successful in the past.

In pricing your product you essentially price from competition but add for every extra feature you have and deduct for the ones you don't. Don't be bashful. Try to be the high price leader. That makes you Number One in the eyes of the consumer and will also give you flexibility in the future to create other products at lower price options for an even larger market segment.

I thought this parable to be quite good relative to pricing: "In medieval England there was a traveling prince who stayed overnight at a country inn. In the morning he had a nice breakfast of eggs. Upon receiving the bill, which was quite high, the prince asked if there was a shortage of eggs in this area. 'No,' replied the innkeeper, 'But there is a shortage of princes!'"

A deer doesn't get hit until it is in your headlights. Be aggressive and go for the jugular to make sure you keep the competition on the defensive and their only thought is survival. This keeps them perpetually off balance. As a consequence, they cannot ever truly focus.

Your competition, to be effective, must be able to match your whole system, which includes technology, good product, marketing, distribution, and service. Manufacturing and quality are actually world-wide commodities today.

If you are attacked, make sure your reaction is extremely fierce but not without integrity. Develop a reputation of, "they go for the jugular and don't take prisoners!" Never treat them as friends. Should you catch them with their shoe laces untied, don't offer to tie them or you are a fool.

Finally, constantly monitor competition, but do not copy them. Copying is for fools!

Core Competency

Core competency is basically that which you do best. It is the sum total of your people and what they know. It is also what others do best, so be aware of and use the core competency of others (distributors and suppliers, for example) to increase the core competency that you already have going for you.

We've seen new management move corporate headquarters so

they could be in a warmer climate or in a more convenient location, but they left the people behind who got them where they are. In these cases, organizations can be wrecked and even fail entirely.

Always remember who *took you to the dance*. In moving our entire company, I was not only scared, I was also concerned about losing our great and skilled teammates. Thus we stayed within a commutable distance with hope that it would work. We lost no one and thus retained our core competency—our people.

Great companies can execute eight to ten competencies simultaneously. Average companies can only do a few. Examples of good competencies might be: sales, marketing, design, development, engineering, finance (which would include leasing), digital technology, people selection, development, and manufacturing. General Electric would be a good example of a company with multiple competencies.

Never forget who you are and what you do best. It's what got you this far.

Partnering

I believe Jim Collins, in his book *Good to Great*, said, "The successful organizations of the future will partner with their competitors."

When Procter & Gamble approached China, it was not as a market to be invaded, but as an opportunity to build new partnerships and develop local capabilities (win: win). The companies that do this are the leaders of the future. Don't let ego get in your way. By working collaboratively, you can increase the size of the pie for everyone.

As a person or company, we all have weaknesses. To survive in any situation, admit your weaknesses and find your needed strength in a counterpart person or company. Everyone will appreciate being part of the successful end result. For some reason, I think competition brings out the best in products and the worst in people. By partnering, we can hopefully bring out the best in both.

PART SEVEN:
PHILOSOPHICAL THINKING

Personal

"As you grow, you become more of who you really are," says Marcus Buckingham. So if you haven't done so already, teach yourself to be neat in everything you do. While in college, I was always a car junkie. I took a night course on engines at a vocational school. I'll never forget the instructor's opening words: "Be neat or you'll be a failure!" That goes for everything in life. When in doubt, dress up, not down.

Build on your strengths. Then add to them. If you're shy, do not turn down invitations. Be glad when you don't know anyone at a social event, as it forces you to meet new people. Your image of yourself, good or bad, comes from the feedback you receive, such as, compliments, promotions, board seats, and invitations. My mother said it best: "God gave you what you have—not to just have it—but to see what you will do with it."

Keep track of what you do and say. Watch your thoughts; they become words. Watch your words; they become actions. Watch your actions; they become habits. Watch your habits; they become character. Watch your character; it becomes your destiny. The author Victor Frankl said in his most wonderful book, *Man's Search for Meaning*, "You can't control what happens to you, but you can control your response to it."

Many times over the years, I have watched people who worked for me make tough decisions that hurt people. Many of these decisions were ones I disagreed with. I knew, however, if I intervened to reverse their decisions, those managers would no longer feel in charge and would lose confidence. Too, all future decisions would be dumped at my feet. When you manage people, you want them to grow and feel like an important part of the organization.

Outside of the company, I've watched many people who were very selfish have more than their share of *bad karma*. I wonder why? People or organizations that are driven by the wrong emotion (such as, hatred, greed, anger, spite or too much ego) are bound to fail.

A person's greatness is determined by their service to mankind. This can happen in a variety of ways. I always feel that reducing inequity is the most positive thing you can do for mankind, in whatever way you choose.

The former CEO of Southwest Airlines, Howard Putnam, had this to say: "The key question to ask yourself when looking in the mirror is, 'Am I really the person my dog thinks I am?'"

Luck

Every successful person or organization has had some lucky breaks along the way. In our case the major lower-end player sold their organization to what was then known as American Hospital Supply. Our distributors (dealers) fought against AHS, since American Hospital Supply was the distributors' competitor. This created a major opening for Midmark.

Then the major high-end competitor, Ritter, began making many strategic errors. They eventually folded. We purchased a segment of *their* business, which put us in a very high and dominate market share position. Although we had great, hardworking people, those two breaks were not created by us. They were pure luck.

If you are alert, you can make your own luck. (Always hit your *best* ball over tough water.) I am not a superstitious person, but I do believe in reincarnation. An Eastern religion term that I've always liked is *karma*. It's a Hindu and Buddhist word describing the force generated by a person's actions to determine his destiny in his next existence. Although reincarnation is a subject too deep to cover here, I do feel karma can carry lifetime to lifetime and can actually be created. How? By living your life in a way that is helpful to humanity. This can increase your chances for *good karma.*

Believe in God

I care not which religion you practice or if you are an agnostic or an atheist, but I see myself reaping deep benefits from my own spiritual awareness. For humans, it seems that it is important to have a *touchstone*—something to go to, rally around, and soothe you when you are down.

Once, while in Sydney, Australia, I was absolutely alone. So I decided to go to a Catholic church on Sunday morning. As the mass ended, I realized I was not really alone at all. The people I saw there, I believe, would have come to my aid if I needed it. It eased the feeling of too much solitude.

Another time, I read a novel about a Polish Jewish couple who had gone through hell during the four years of World War II. As a result, the couple clearly doubted organized religion and even questioned the existence of a God. So they developed a pattern of praying to their mothers who had always been there for them in life and were an emotional haven during the terrible times of World War II. It was a love of which they were certain—a touchstone.

Dostoevsky once stated, "If there is no God, then all things are permissible." Winston Churchill, with an eye on the Nazis and Communism, observed, "You leave out God and you substitute the devil."

Whether you are an atheist, an agnostic, or a person of faith, it may be interesting to hear, as I have, that people with a connection to a religious community tend to have a better sense of well being and are generally happier than those who don't. Perhaps it has something to do with social interaction. I do not know the answer. However, for me, it does work and makes me feel good about who I am. I remember going to the hospital to see our first grandchild. This tiny creature, so perfect, so dear—something had to create this incredible masterpiece!

I recently received this via e-mail: A grammar school class was asked to write down the Seven Wonders of the World. As the teacher read different papers that mentioned such wonders as the Taj Mahal, the pyramids, China's Great Wall, etc., she noticed one little girl was still writing. When asked why she hadn't finished yet, she said, "Because there are so many wonders." But here are *my* seven: "To see, to hear, to taste, to touch, to feel, to laugh, and to love!" What an insightful child! Her wonders weren't built or conceived by man, but they are a heck of a lot more important.

Some years ago, when I was watching the Olympics on television, a young, female athlete of Mormon faith was asked how she managed to come in first. Her answer: "You just do your best and then it is up to God."

In conclusion, I reiterate: It doesn't matter which religion you practice or if you are an atheist or an agnostic, but I personally reap deep benefits from my own spiritual awareness.

Philosophically Speaking

While looking for and designing our tombstone, Esther and I looked at many cemeteries and found a rather simple tombstone which we liked at Lakeview Cemetery in Cleveland. That is the cemetery where John D. Rockefeller has his tomb and family plot. I noted to myself that the people with the small tombstones were just as dead as the Rockefellers under their huge tombstone. Death is a real leveler, figuratively *and* literally.

I take comfort in reading the wisdom of others I admire. Their words are often my exact thoughts before I have thought them! Take James Allen, from *As A Man Thinkest*: "Good thoughts and actions never produce bad results and bad thoughts and actions can never produce good results."

Or from the philosopher Lao-Tze: "He who knows much about others may be knowledgeable, but he who understands himself is much more intelligent. They who control others may be powerful, but those who master themselves are mightier, still."

There are many well-known quotes from famous philosophers that I could list here, but you have likely read them elsewhere. And although I'm not a philosopher, I do have some philosophical thoughts every once in a while:

Want to feel rich? Count all the things that you have that money can't, or didn't, buy.

If you get up one day and feel rotten, the best thing you can do is to phone or email several friends, genuinely compliment them and cheer them up. It will make *you* feel terrific, as well.

Planning on getting even with someone? If so, you are only letting that person continue to hurt you.

Get rich slowly. You'll enjoy life more and sleep better. And don't forget, at the end of the day, you'll still be rich.

In 2003, an East Coast venture capital group with whom I had become partner, sold two companies. Because of this, I did extremely well, financially. I could have easily bought the most expensive Mercedes or Porsche. I decided that wouldn't make me happy. Instead, Esther and I set up a charitable trust from which we have received enormous enjoyment.

Besides, as I once read, "You can't have everything. Where would you put it?"

Children

The reason youth is so wonderful is because the young don't yet realize the complexity of life. However, the sooner they are set on a path of having to support and decide for themselves, the sooner they will become aware of the complexities. A good thing to remember is, *the more you give them, the more you take away.*

Children who never hear, "No," won't be able to say, "No." My parents told me, and we passed on to our children, "If you have a problem at school and get your tail kicked, when you get home it'll be kicked again!"

For strength of character, your child should be allowed to make mistakes on their own turf and figure out how to get out of them. Teach them it is all right to fail but not all right to quit.

As your children grow up, read to them, around them, and with them. Let them see lots of books in your home. And by restricting television hours, they'll become more creative. A trip to the library will become more meaningful to them than a trip to McDonald's. We have always felt that a child who reads can work his or her way out of most problems.

On a personal note, Esther and I both grew up in comfortable surroundings, but neither set of parents ever saw the inside of a country club or a Cadillac. Having four children in eight years was a physical and somewhat financial challenge for Esther and me, but we wanted our children to grow up with a thirst for adventure and knowledge. We bought a travel trailer and we spent two weeks each year having adventures like digging clams in Nova Scotia and enjoying rodeos in Gillette, Wyoming. These things stimulated their curiosity, and now they also have wanderlust in spades. To this day, they love to reminisce about those trips. You, as a person, are the sum total of all your past experiences. Make them interesting and you make yourself interesting.

I like what Warren Buffett said about his children: "I gave them just enough capital to do something, but not enough to do nothing."

Finally, it is not who you were or what you have done, but what you have left behind.

Our family at our 50th wedding anniversery, 2007. Our children: Mitch, standing second from left; Josh, far right; Polly, seated third from left; Anne, second from right.

Class

Classy people are not just friendly to their competitors but friendly to everyone. Classy people never show anger. Classy people have *manners*.

If you think someone doesn't like you, continue to be friendly. I remember a customer we courted who treated us rudely. We became twice as friendly and never once allowed underhandedness with our competitor to enter our mind. That thought would have caused us to be unfocused and perhaps generate anger among us, which would have been destructive to ourselves. Conversely, we've seen a supplier who lost their business with us become angry and resentful toward us. That built a wall between us.

I once created a metaphor of a home that has burned completely down, but the chimney still stands. The chimney is your *class*. Things can happen around you, but your *class* always stands.

Dave Bester, a retired vice president from Midmark, once said, "You get a good for a good and a bad for a bad." I learned a lot from his statement. We've never sued anyone, and it is not our intention to do so.

What is class? I found this somewhere, and it goes like this:

"• Class never runs scared. It is sure-footed and confident in the knowledge that one can meet life head-on and handle whatever comes along.

• Class never makes excuses. It takes its lumps and learns from past mistakes.

• Class is being considerate of others. It knows that good manners are nothing more than a series of petty sacrifices.

• Class bespeaks an aristocracy that has nothing to do with ancestors or money. The most affluent blueblood can be totally without class while the descendant of a Welsh miner may ooze class from every pore.

- Class never tries to build itself up by tearing others down.
- Class is already up and need not strive to look better by making others look worse.
- Class can 'walk with kings and keep its virtue and talk with crowds and keep the common touch.' Everyone is comfortable with the person who has class because he is comfortable with himself. If you have class, you don't need much of anything else. If you don't have it, no matter what else you have—it doesn't make much difference."

—Signed, Anonymous.

The following is *my* definition of being classy (mannerly) that I wrote for our children and grandchildren. Class is:

- going to social functions and smiling through them even though you prefer not to be there.
- treating ladies like ladies.
- ladies acting like ladies and gentlemen acting like gentlemen.
- learning to mask true feelings.
- being hurt and not allowing anyone to know it.
- not *always* saying what's on your mind.
- patiently removing yourself from a situation without hurting anyone's feelings.
- pulling people together versus dividing them.
- never being greedy or selfish; it is sharing and giving.
- never complaining but patiently accepting and acting evenly always.
- never stooping to talking about people or gossiping.
- talking of ideas, things, etc.

- saying something good or not saying anything at all.
- never standing in judgment; that belongs to God.
- giving a gift to a party hostess, writing thank you notes, and returning phone calls within 24 hours (e-mails don't count).
- inviting people back and returning favors, but class is never expecting invitations or favors to be returned.
- never being a garbage mouth.
- maybe dressing in out-of-date clothes, but they are always neat and clean.
- patiently apologizing when a wrong action or words come up.
- never leaving an event early.
- being patient.
- thanking the speaker after the event.
- realizing that *being classy* is more important than anything else except God and love.

Finally, from the author Ralph W. Sockmon: "Nothing is so strong as gentleness, and nothing is so gentle as real strength."

Now *that's* class.

Creativity

When our children were very young, we brought home one of their most prized and fun toys. It was a huge cardboard box. It just made their creativity gush.

Being poor can bring out the creativity in us. This story is to prove my point: Early on, we bought a line of equipment from American Metal Furniture. We saw that *their* plant had an automated, wet paint system that must have cost a fortune.

We knew that one of these systems was necessary for efficient manufacturing in order to compete, especially in the manufacturing of drawers, which were the high volume item. But we didn't have the money to buy a similar piece of equipment for our plant.

John Oldiges, a young engineer we tapped to head our engineering department, came back from lunch one day and said, "I may have the solution to the drawers." He had noticed the drawers in his dresser at home were plastic. He researched and eventually found their source, and ultimately, even had them molded for us in the same color as our equipment. That saved our bacon!

On the sales circuit, we would pull our truck into a dealer's parking lot, and during the demonstration, we would pull the drawers out of the table. We would then point out the advantage of having no rust to worry about, and easy-to-clean rounded corners. We even stood on them to exhibit how strong they were. Eventually, the whole medical industry switched to all plastic drawers.

John Oldiges went further with his low-budget, creative genius and developed a welded slide instead of an expensive machined mechanical slide for our power table movements. This gave us a great cost advantage over our competition, and again, was driven by our inability to machine, as we couldn't afford the mill we needed. Creativity saved us great expense.

Ken Lagone, a successful, retired G.E. director, explained his success: "I had a major advantage. I was raised poor." And, that is a major, major advantage! Necessity is the mother of invention.

A good question to ask yourself is: "Are we succeeding by cutting or creating?" You must create before you can cut. It doesn't take superior skill to cut, but it does to create.

And know that it is one hundred times easier to keep costs down rather than to bring them down.

Culture

Initially, I was reluctant to write this book because I thought I'd be giving our company secrets away. Then Don Kitzmiller, our former vice president of sales, convinced me that the competition can copy some things, but they can't copy the entire culture. Any strong culture cannot be cloned.

Make your culture so strong that people who don't fit in will leave, and outsiders learning of it may like what they hear, decide to be a part of your culture as a teammate, and stay for a long time.

What is corporate culture anyway? A broad definition is an unwavering set of beliefs, values, and relationships that guide the decisions of a company to achieve its goals. There are dozens of ways Midmark expresses its corporate culture on a daily basis. Here are a few:

We have put on some zany presentations at trade shows for over twenty-five years. A few of these were: dressing all of the sales people in wedding dresses; as Santa and elves; as Romans; and as Blues Brothers, to name a few. They certainly stood out and we had fun doing it. Too, we like to have a family member present at every major trade show. It shows a particular kind of care, on our part, and the competition thinks, "Why aren't our owners here?"

We built our new plant in Versailles, Ohio, in 1970. Afterwards, we were approached by the Versailles Development Association, who said there was a larger organization interested in relocating to Versailles and asked if we would we write a letter citing the wonderful labor, business climate, etc. We had chosen Versailles in 1969, because there were no unions there and no other manufacturing plants. Driving home that night I thought, "That is probably the dumbest thing we could do!" However, after sleeping on it, we told ourselves the honorable thing to do would be to write the letter, which we did. Well, that new organization built a beautiful, large plant right across from us on seventeen acres. It was the Argosy Division of Airstream Trailers owned by Beatrice Foods, and they offered better wages and better fringe benefits than we did, as we were quite small at the time.

However, in the late '70s, a fuel crisis hit and gasoline became quite expensive. They pulled the main switch on the Argosy plant, and it stood idle for two years or so.

Their building and plant's selling price kept coming down. We floated a $3 million bond, which we believed was actually more than our combined net worth. We added cranes and a major office addition, sold our 1915 factory and proceeded to move desks, inventory, files, and all our large machines to the new location. Bill Coomer, our vice president of manufacturing, headed the project, and we shut down on a Thursday and opened the next Monday morning in the new building. Bill did his usual good job and it went quite smoothly. Naturally, we were very concerned about losing business, people quitting, maybe getting a union, but it worked out quite well. Psychologically, our people felt ten feet tall, because we had been stuffed into a building on a poor street behind a huge organization and we never got to see the sun until 10 a.m. as the large company was east of us. Now we had a new plant and office and we could see the sun at 6 a.m.

My point in telling the story is in doing the right thing (values, beliefs, and relationships) by responding positively to the Versailles Development Association's request, rather than being selfish and ignoring it, ended up as a major step in setting our culture for the future.

A few years later, we were able to buy a major trucking organization's office contiguous to our new plant. It had a very nice office and, with the extra acreage, it gave us a campus-like appearance. We now had seventy-eight acres. Having made all these moves at very good prices set the stage for our strong balance sheet, and our approach to future investments.

The same goes for new CEOs. If they want change and cooperation, and if they need to make changes and gain cooperation, they had better learn the culture of an organization and work within that framework. This goes for mergers and acquisitions that start with strategic analysis. It then moves into financial analysis. If these two work out, the players become pretty excited. The last thing on the table is culture analysis. This is where, perhaps, it should have been to start with. The obvious problem is you can't number-crunch culture. As a backdrop for the above, bear in mind that the success rate for major, life-changing mergers (not acquisitions) is only one in ten.

Another example of our very personal beliefs, values, and relationships (culture) occurred when there was an omission found by our tax preparer some years ago. One day our tax preparer called and said he found that we had missed reporting $10,000 of income on our personal returns from an earlier tax return. Our attorney who prepared our taxes, along with Esther and me, had all missed this omission. We were told that we had only three days and then it would be outside of the time statute. We told our tax preparer to send in our amendment, and we would pay it. Our choice was to be honest, because after all, we reap all the benefits that our taxes pay for, like anyone else. Although no one knew it at the time, it was a cultural cornerstone.

Ego

Humility is a basic ingredient of leadership. In fact, I feel it is the highest quality and greatest asset of a leader. I've seen egos destroy more companies than competition ever will.

In terms of ego, or excess pride, we've seen the refusal to apologize destroy dozens of relationships, including marriages, families, careers, and friendships. What a pitiful loss for the lack of just a few simple words. Being able to admit you are wrong is a sign of strength. Apologizing or expressing regret is like a confessional. You immediately let go of the past and feel good about yourself. It builds relationships instead of destroying them.

When we set up our family foundation to do charitable work, we called it Bocholt Foundation, after the town in Germany where our family was from. In later years I asked our children if they would want to change it to the Eiting Foundation. I was quite proud of their response. They felt having our name on something was not important to them. Doing charitable work was their only desire.

I have always subscribed to the thinking, "Don't call attention to yourself." The Japanese have another way to express that thought: "A nail that sticks up gets hammered down."

This brings two things to mind. Where we first lived, I was a driving force in starting the library. Prior to that, I actually saved someone's life. This deed was witnessed by others, but neither of these deeds was ever trumpeted.

To bring that home, when we broke ground for our first medical plant in 1969, I was there but not in the photo of the groundbreaking. I wanted the credit to go to our people.

Correspondingly, when the brochure came out for our 75th anniversary, one of our vice presidents complained to me that a personal quote he sent in was not included. I responded, "At least you got your picture in it," as mine was not.

Shortly after we got our first jet, Esther and I flew to make a requested appearance in New Orleans. Right before they started the engines, I said to the pilots, "Be extra careful, you've got some expensive freight back here." The copilot turned to me and responded, "You've got some expensive freight up here, too!" I guess I deserved that.

We have been strong supporters of Direct Relief International (DRI), a wonderful charitable organization that supplies the world with medical equipment and medicine ($200 million worth a year). I actually term-limited out from their board of directors, but I am still connected through our son, Mitch. The president of DRI is Thomas Tighe, who has done a great job of leading and building the organization. He was invited by Santa Barbara City College to give a lecture on self-esteem, and Esther and I attended. Well, he showed up to speak wearing jeans, and I thought to myself, "Here is a man with tremendous self-esteem and no ego!" I was right on both counts.

On our first trip to England, the bus stopped in a tiny village. We got out and walked down an alley to a small cemetery. Our guide pointed out a tombstone the same size as the others. It read Winston Churchill.

Yiddish proverb: "You don't stumble because you are weak, but because you think yourself strong."

I have done much public speaking for over forty years. I constantly caution myself to never forget that it is about the audience and not myself. I introduce myself as a farmer who got lucky.

I like what Will Rogers said: "No man is great if he thinks he is."

Or, as they say in Texas: "Big hat. No cows."

Etc.

You can't pick your parents and you'll never get over them, good, bad or indifferent.

We all are the sum total of all our experiences. Your DNA, your parents, your experiences are indelible—hopefully, the result is a gestalt you can be proud of.

As I see it, when placing yourself in a job, you can be paid in one of two currencies. One is cash and the other a strong experience. My advice is to take to the experience and that experience will be most rewarded by working for a strong and tough boss. By taking the strong experience, the cash will catch up to you eventually.

Bear in mind that you have a fairly defined twenty-five year time span to truly become a real success. Generally, it is when one is between the ages of 30 and 55. Just make darned sure you are doing what you do best during those years.

The key to a happy and successful career is to find out what you are really, really good at doing, to enjoy and do more of that, and less of other things. Find your passion! The best place to be to get where you truly want to go, is where you are.

Family Business

I once read that family-owned companies make up 89 percent of all businesses and 35 percent of Fortune 500 companies. Only 30 percent of family businesses make it to the second generation, and only 10 percent to the third; 3 percent to the fourth. At that point, if the family gets some decent counseling and a strong board, the percentage goes up to approximately 15 percent. These numbers aren't mine, but from experience, I bet they are close.

The average age of a business is twenty-four years. At about the fourth generation, the family begins to realize it is not about capital or product but about the development and mentorship of the family. A professional, outside board is extremely important at this point, and it also needs to act somewhat as a family facilitator.

The first generation is naturally focused on the customer for survival. The customer *is* the reason for its existence. With the second generation, that begins to slip away. The third generation, many times, is too focused on itself, personally, to survive.

One advantage of a family organization is that it provides immediate focus for the eligible presidential candidate. It also eliminates the necessity for the candidate to make a career choice. However, it can be dangerous if the true passion for the business isn't there. The candidate may have to face a frustrating lifetime of doing what someone else wanted them to do instead of making their own career choice.

Family stakeholders are very precious—even third generation ones. There is an old Hebrew saying that goes, "I'd rather have them in my tent peeing out, than outside peeing in!" Keep relationships intact. It'll pay big dividends. The majority of businesses are failures as a result of lack of trust and communication among family members.

At a World Presidential Meeting in Peru several years ago, we met a really neat guy from Iowa. We asked him the age of his organization and he *apologetically* stated that it was started by his father. Having just enough wine to be extremely emphatic, I said, "For gosh sake, Bob, you can't pick your parents! It's what you do with what God gave you that counts." I think he came away feeling much better about himself.

As Midmark grew, we realized we had the option of going public. Another option was to simply say "Yes" to our many suitors. *Fortunately,* we said no to both. In talking to the many people we knew who went public or sold, we couldn't find one that was truly happy. Distilling it down further, we saw the only advantage of going public or selling out is that it would simply provide money. But money is not an end in itself; it is simply a means to one. Our balance sheet was strong, we were strategically positioned correctly, and we had the most important ingredient of all—smart, dedicated, and trustworthy people who worked very hard and were having fun. They enjoyed following the vision.

The great advantage we saw in remaining private was our ability to think long term and move quickly. Since we were in a solid industry group, we knew we could keep doing that as far as we could see. Luckily, I have a replacement who is smarter, better educated, and harder-working than I was. If a family can put two dynamic leaders back-to-back, you might have a sixty-year run. You can really *move the needle* in sixty years.

Also, there are great tax advantages. Just a few, depending on whether you are a C or S Corp might be: You can build net worth without being taxed; perhaps a strong base salary; and the ability to own things privately and lease them back to the corporation. There are many others based on the situation.

A privately held organization forces a discipline on the owners that must be continually addressed. Like a farmer, they have a high liquid net worth, a good income, and have to answer to no one but their family. A darned good life it can be if you respect the family.

One last, final, personal note: My father had been retired for some time, was dying from a brain tumor, and I was called to the hospital late one night only to see that the monitor had flat-lined.

He was gone. That was a very defining moment for me. Even though he had been far away from the business for several years, I had always felt that if something did not go right, we would still share the blame. At that moment, I knew, there was no place to hide. It was me and me, alone…a very maturing moment.

A paragraph worth inserting here is the tenuous value of shares held in a private company. I have read in more than one text that minority shares are typically valued at 40 to 50 percent of the actual book value. It is caveat emptor and be sure to have a buy/sell agreement in writing should you decide to invest.

From the corporation's standpoint, my advice is to make sure your shareholders always have an exit window available to them. If not, too often shares end up in the wrong hands, which has made many CEOs' lives miserable.

Friends

My mother told me many times, "When you die, if you can say you have one true friend, you will be lucky indeed." I truly believe that. Don't be fooled. We all have acquaintances who only call us when they need something. These are not friends, believe me!

Here is my definition of a friend: Someone with whom you are comfortable, have the same interests, and perhaps most important, you can confide in without them taking advantage of the knowledge, or passing it on. You accept each other, warts-and-all, and you can count on each other in good times and bad. The chemistry is definitely there.

Don't worry if your friends eat lunch with their hat on or use salty language. The important thing is you enjoy yourself in their company, and you can act goofy and laugh heartily with them.

I have learned that being thoughtful and giving is the best way to build a relationship. My wife and I have many friends who are tight when it comes to spending money, but we've learned to overlook that because of their loyalty. But loyalty is only one important component of a relationship. Distilling it down, you have to give in order to get. Train yourself to think of others first.

Yiddish proverb: Better one old friend than two new. For instance, I have a good friend with whom I have gone fishing with for fifty-five years. We see each other only once a year, and it's as if we have not been apart—like old wine, our friendship is very, very good.

When we first began building the organization to be what it is today, we were able to entice about seven people away from a NYSE company. These folks had the know-how and experience to be key to our operation. The president of that company and I later developed a strong relationship and have since traveled the world together for thirty-five years. Had I been he, I might have become angered over losing seven good employees to us. Today, I am thankful for his wisdom in allowing our deep friendship to develop.

Yiddish proverb: He who loses money, loses much. He, who loses a friend, loses much more.

Give to Receive

I was very fortunate to have parents who taught me the joy of giving. During World War II, my father had a 1940 Plymouth coupe. Its only seat was a bench in the front, but it had a very long trunk. Every Christmas Eve afternoon, he and I would go to the grocery store and fill as many boxes as we could fit into the trunk with bread, sausage, pancake mix, and even Log Cabin syrup in cans shaped like a log cabin. There were other items such as candy, as well. We would then go to the homes of the very poorest people in our village, and I would open the trunk and carry a box to each home.

Can you imagine a better legacy to leave a child? Wasn't I lucky to have such a wonderful experience and generous parents?

Another person who impacted me tremendously was a brilliant engineer by the name of Rueben Wissman. He was not formally educated, but he had a very successful career with many important patents. When he retired, I began to visit him in the evenings as I knew he was a fountain of knowledge. He told me that when he initially retired he would sit around and feel sorry for himself. Then he decided he would do pro bono (free) engineering work for the village of New Bremen where he lived. It made him feel fulfilled and appreciated. This really shored up my philosophy of giving.

Our organization has always been very giving, not just charitably, but also in sharing knowledge to compatible organizations. We have found that to be the hallmark of any successful organization.

Midmark has a close relationship with Johnson & Johnson through Direct Relief International. Though Johnson & Johnson has done much more than Midmark over the years, we have donated millions of dollars of current, obsolete, and trade-in equipment to them for shipments worldwide. They are usually the first ones arriving in areas destroyed by earthquakes, tornadoes, and other natural disasters. I spent about ten years as a board member until my term limit ran out. I was also successful in getting other organizations, such as Miltex Instruments, to donate. I was a board member for them, as well. They gave a huge donation of medical and dental instruments. My brother, Jack, and his wife, Marie, have also been major financial supporters of Direct Relief International, plus many, many other charities. They are good people!

How do you pay back a mentor who has everything already? You can give support to their children or grandchildren, build self-esteem and mentor them in return. You can open business or professional doors for them. Another great way of showing your appreciation is to support their favorite charities.

The greatest thing anyone can do for humanity is to provide people with the opportunity for a job. It not only provides income, but dignity and self-esteem. Don't just *give* them the fish. Give them what they need to catch their *own* fish.

Our family does not expect rewards for giving. Giving is the reward. No one needs to know who gave it. Here again, the 80/20 rule applies. For every dollar or hour you give, you'll receive four.

Happiness

Happiness is not a place; it is a state of mind. In our case, our happiness comes from giving and not receiving. Receiving is a fleeting emotion, whereas giving has longevity. It sticks with you a long time.

Happiness does not come from having your name on a building; it comes from helping people build a career in order to be self-sustaining. It makes you happy because you've helped them to be happy and to feel good about themselves.

My wife, Esther, sometimes wonders why I get emotional with a leap of faith for someone or something. It is simply that I strongly remember when we were struggling and people took a chance on us. You never forget these things.

I've said many times, "If I'm not happy, I don't know about it." So what's it all about, anyhow? So many people get wrapped up in *things* as a route to happiness. Happiness isn't in *things*. Happiness can be anywhere and everywhere. Some of my examples are:

- One person who truly loves you
- Family
- The look on your dog's face when you come home from work
- Sitting on the porch and watching the rain
- A long walk
- A perfect tack on your sailboat
- The feeling after detailing your sports car
- Nice friends who, after you have made a fool of yourself, don't feel you've done a permanent job of it
- Giving your time, talent, or treasure and seeing the results it created
- A completed project on the job
- A low golf score

I once read, "Money cannot buy happiness, but happiness can buy money!" Happiness isn't getting what you want, it is wanting what you have. And a smile is an inexpensive way to improve your looks. This isn't mine, but I love it. "In life, have some fun, make some coins, and leave some footprints in the sand."

The happiest person is usually not the one who has the most, but the one who needs the least.

Health

Our son-in-law Dr. Rob Klamar likes to paraphrase Ben Franklin: "Everything in moderation, including moderation." Personally, I feel the mental part of us drives the physical. In addition to exercise, proper diet, rest, etc., the key is to stay mentally challenged and very busy. Work is very, very good for people.

From a physical standpoint, I feel getting a dog is one of the healthiest things a person can do. Why? Like a child, they require care, and thus, you keep from getting selfish. Physically, however, they expect a daily walk. That has always kept me in good shape. It is a win-win situation, and if you get a dog from a shelter, it is win, win, win!

I think my rule of sixes is quite good: "Always be up by 6 a.m. (the time to make donuts) and *never* consume anything alcoholic before 6 p.m. (the time to relax)."

The people around me whom I watch getting old, have decided to get old. They no longer want to do challenging things (i.e. learn, travel, read, meet new people). Personally, I feel they are boring. My wife Esther and I are continually taking classes about different subjects. It really keeps us on our toes. I find when I speak at Westmont College in Santa Barbara, California, or at the University of Dayton, the young people are smart and ambitious. They continually challenge me and force me, for instance, to keep up with industry reading.

The following advice will add years to your life: Interact with lots of people, especially the young. Give time, talent, or treasure and pursue plans for the things mentioned above. There is nothing like jumping out of bed each morning knowing that this day has a purpose. It will keep you optimistic and add years to your life.

Don't be a hermit. Interaction with people (all kinds) is what keeps you young.

In 2015, Midmark will be 100 years old. I like to dream about being pushed onto the stage, slobbering in my wheelchair, releasing those hundred white doves, and thanking God for all of the wonderful teammates who have brought us this far.

Finally, though getting a bit *long in the tooth*, we feel *what grows, never grows old*. Keep looking ahead optimistically. We think that the years from 60 to 70 were the best decade for us. We had coins in our pockets, our children were raised, and we still had our health and flexibility.

Integrity

In the final analysis, integrity is really your best asset. It is your rudder and your true moral compass in striving for the pursuit of success and happiness. During a conversation with money manager Ken Fisher, who writes for *Forbes* magazine, I asked him, "In the final analysis, what is the one thing that you look for in a company?" His answer was, "Honesty." Either you are honest or you aren't. There are no gray areas.

Integrity is like virginity; you can only lose it once. You cannot only tell one lie because you have to keep creating new ones to cover the one you just told. Plus, the trust someone had in you will be lost forever. *A promise made is a promise kept.*

Steven Covey says, "The future organizations will require high-trust cultures to survive globally. You can't change an organization's culture in one weekend. It took G.E.'s Jack Welch eleven years to do it." In the final analysis you don't really work for an organization, you work for the values of its leaders.

I once played golf with a man and noticed he did not count all of his strokes. Some years later he asked me to invest with him on a project, and I quickly found he did not count all the money either. Point being, you can't be one-half or three-fourths honest. Either you are or you aren't.

Herb Score, major league pitcher and sports broadcaster, presented a poem that I found quite worthy of repeating:

The Man in the Glass (by Dale Wimbrow)
When you get what you want in your struggle for pelf,
And the world makes you King for a day,
Then go to the mirror and look at yourself,
And see what that guy has to say.

For it isn't your father or mother or wife,
Whose judgment upon you must pass.
The feller whose verdict counts most in your life
Is the guy staring back from the glass.

He's the fellow to please, never mind all the rest,
For he's with you clear up to the end,
And you've passed your most dangerous, difficult test
If the guy in the glass is your friend.

You may be like Jack Horner and chisel a plum,
And think you're a wonderful guy,
But the man in the glass says you're only a bum
If you can't look him straight in the eye.

You can fool the whole world down the pathway of years,
And get pats on the back as you pass,
But your final reward will be heartache and tears
If you've cheated the guy in the glass.

The meaning to me is that we must make the best of the ability God has given us. We have to do the things that are right rather than those that make us look good or make us popular. When all is said and done each day, and we put our head on the pillow, it's just us and God, and we can't fool either one.

Last, from Will Rogers: "Lead your life so you wouldn't be afraid to sell the family parrot to the town gossip."

Trust

Of course trust and integrity are intertwined. On one of the first days that my new replacement was on the job, I commented, "You only have to be concerned about five letters, T-R-U-S-T." I could write a whole book on the word and never cover it. It is much too complex, so I'll try to give a few examples.

I never had to worry about personal problems at home when I traveled, because I knew Esther would be there for our children and would make good economic and operating decisions relative to such things as running our home and caring for our children.

From a corporate standpoint, I was very fortunate to have a wonderful executive vice president, Denny Meyer. He and I grew up together, went to the same school, church, and in fact, he married the girl next door to me. We surely had chemistry. In fact, our trust and compatibility were so complete that we could even finish each other's sentences.

Adding to that compatibility, he was accounting based, while I was not, and I was able to trust him to take care of any number-related issues. I also noted his personal decisions prior to joining Midmark, and I thought them to be quite good. The upshot was, he did a great job heading up our operations, and I never had to be concerned that decisions made in my absence would not be good ones. We are great friends to this day and have a monthly luncheon with a group of retired Midmark leaders who call themselves The Roosters.

Our new CEO, Anne Eiting Klamar, had been good at sports, leadership, was very bright and not afraid of tough challenges while getting her degrees. In addition, she married a fellow who is a wonderful physician, and who is conservatively compatible with our family. Combining those ingredients has allowed me to completely trust whatever decisions she makes.

That, of course, makes me a very, very lucky person!

Spouse
✳︎

A few years ago, I was asked by a young single person, "How do you know you have made the right choice when you marry?" My answer was, "She'll inspire you. You'll feel smarter, more secure, and absolutely better about yourself. Your mate for life should increase your self-confidence." Of course, that works both ways between partners.

I married the daughter of a very successful entrepreneur. She could, therefore, accept all the grief I gave her in building my career. She readily accepted things like water in the basement, being snowed-in, and especially, taking full-time care of four children as

I traveled. My wife's ability to relieve me of any worry as I traveled was so very important to me. I was always certain the children were safe and well cared for. The person you marry will have a profound effect on your career.

There never was a crisis she couldn't work her way out of when I was gone, whether it was water in the basement, a non-starting car, or a school problem. I was very fortunate to marry a woman who understood that the organization was always foremost on the horizon. She was always there with a cocktail or dinner party when needed, or a dinner out with customers or interviewees. The food was always good, the house immaculate, and the kids mannerly. If we found we had a convention or meeting appearance she was always flexible and quick to pack.

About seven years ago, we looked at an organization in Malaysia. Because of the circumstances at the time, Esther and I discussed it and volunteered to move there for the first six months to build our culture into it. That gives you some idea of her passion and dedication to the organization.

A spouse need not be an employee to be a valuable part of an organization. If he or she believes in you, he or she will thus believe in the organization. Her presence always meant a lot to everyone, especially me.

Here is another bit of wisdom: "The difference between a successful marriage and a mediocre one consists of daily leaving three or four things left unsaid." My wife and I have celebrated fifty years of marriage. That's a lot of unsaid material.

Socrates had this to say about marriage: "By all means marry. If you get a good wife, you'll become happy; if you get a bad one, you'll become a philosopher."

PART EIGHT:
THE FUTURE

Education

A good education creates a platform for what you must learn after you have graduated. It is not to answer questions; it is to prepare you to ask them and also to behave differently. It is precisely designed to correct the instincts of human nature.

Although my initial education was *light*, indeed, I did follow it with two advanced management programs at the University of Cincinnati. This was followed by my intense interest in Young Presidents and that is quite a finishing school in itself. To this moment, I am constantly in courses and seminars, besides being a very prolific reader and a guest lecturer at different universities, which I truly enjoy the most. The young people continually challenge me and it forces a discipline on me of staying current on all things.

Although I feel good about all the above, I pale next to our CEO Anne Eiting Klamar. She shares my thirst for knowledge and spends up to three weeks a year at Harvard University. This keeps her current and has given her very valuable contacts throughout the world. And though I am merely *drafting* behind her, she continues to inspire me as well.

Midmark is very fortunate to have a leader of her breadth, leadership capability, and knowledge that has come from intense, formal education.

Wisdom

There is a huge difference between knowing something and understanding it. An education does not give you either real-life experience or wisdom. To understand something you have to live it and feel it. Conversely, good judgment comes from experience and a lot of that comes from bad judgment! Wisdom is a strong component of what you've learned from failures. Failure isn't shameful. It is the greatest teacher of all.

A dull person doesn't know what they don't know.

Anyone will know that you must move your pieces forward in chess. That is knowledge. Intelligence is deciding which ones and where. Thus, life's successes or failures are based on decisions that are intelligent or not.

Older people are more interesting and knowledgeable. They've simply seen more. One thing I like about getting older is that I understand more. I'm able to put all the pieces together.

I have a metaphor about wisdom as altitude. I feel you climb 10,000 feet each ten career years. After forty years (40,000 feet), you can really see the inter-relationship of many parts, ideas, and pieces.

I feel the hallmark of intelligence is the intensity and focus while asking many questions (two ears, one mouth). Also, I have always noticed that someone with a PhD will usually answer a question with another question. I feel they do this to gather more information. That is wise in itself.

Do things you are afraid of and you'll no longer be afraid. You'll end up stronger and smarter. Your true potential will be realized only if you continually push and test yourself into new unfamiliar situations.

Marilyn Vos Savant, who wrote about wisdom in *Parade* magazine, said, "To acquire knowledge, one must study; to acquire wisdom, one must observe." Wisdom has much to do about knowing one's self. Wisdom requires mistakes and seeing how you'll react to them.

Change

Look for changes. They usually create opportunity and the greater the changes, the more the opportunites.

Jim Collins of Stanford University said, "A crisis is a terrible thing to waste." In a crisis, it is easier to execute changes. In a crisis, people accept change faster. Most change is good. That is why entrepreneurial organizations do better, in terms of change, than established ones. They accept change as a way of life because they know they must keep probing and changing as they are seeking success. They do, however, know success is out there somewhere.

Extreme change requires a deep, mutual trust with your employees, suppliers, distributors, and customers. The quality of these relationships is very, very important. You need people who can think together and trust each other in the process.

The best way to control change is to create it. And the great excitement of the future is that we can shape it. If you truly want extreme change, chances are you'll have to change some of your people. If you have *rearview mirror* people, it is not going to happen. You want to keep your employees strong enough to embrace the future with the change. People entrenched in the past way of doing things will feel threatened, therefore, they must go.

Jack Welch of G.E. gave us this gem: "When the rate of change inside an organization becomes slower than the rate of change in the marketplace, the end is in sight."

In new situations, the newcomer has a surprising advantage because they don't have *baggage*. They can move faster and focus more clearly. That was a great advantage we had when entering the medical industry.

Don't just rest on past successes. Keep your intellectual capital focused on moving forward and trying new things, or eventually those past successes become mere *husks* of what they were in the past. The formulas for yesterday's success are usually formulas for failure tomorrow.

Every organization has to prepare for the abandonment of everything it does. Linear thinking is useless in the non-linear world that we live in today. Many times it takes total abandonment of what you have been doing. That is the only way you can pour a new footer from which to build a new foundation. It goes without saying that very strong leadership is required.

And, if you don't think change is inevitable, look at these statistics from 1907:

The average life expectancy in the U.S. was 47 years old.

Only 14 percent of the homes in the U.S. had a bathtub.

Only 8 percent of the homes had a telephone.

There were only 8,000 cars in the U.S., and only 144 miles of paved roads.

Alabama, Mississippi, Iowa, and Tennessee were each more heavily populated than California.

The average wage in the U.S. was 22 cents per hour.

The average U.S. worker made between $200 and $400 per year.

Only 6 percent of all Americans had graduated from high school.

There were about 230 reported murders in the entire United States.

Just try to imagine what it may be like in another hundred years. It staggers the mind!

Decisions

If you have a tough decision to make, take time to think it through from all angles. Yet, just because you have a month to make that decision, don't stall. You don't want lose an opportunity because of sitting on the fence too long. Paradoxically, do not ever rush a decision. Gather as much data that is available. Last-minute acquired data has saved many careers and billions of dollars.

Empirical or gut decisions are dangerous because they raid the reason of doing hard statistical research. From Andy Grove, CEO of Intel: "Drive deep into the data, then trust your gut." Short-term solutions many times create long-terms problems. We have always worked on the premise that when stumped, make your decision as if you were a public company even though you aren't.

Yogi Berra said a mouthful: "When you come to a fork in the road, take it." (When asked if he wanted his pizza cut into four or eight slices he said, "Four. I don't think I can eat eight.")

You might think you can't get hurt by not taking a chance, but we guarantee you'll miss 100 percent of the opportunities on the chances you didn't take. Risk is a major ingredient of success. And it's fun!

Future

You create your own future. It just doesn't happen by itself. If it has thus far, you've been lazy! Your thoughts today should be focused on tomorrow, not yesterday. If they are on yesterday, you are old!

If you're a visionary and a leader, today's results were created by yesterday's plans. Your future beyond that will be determined by your vision...and you had better have one.

Tomorrow will be fun. Yesterday is boring.

Grow your thinking power. We can see our new president of Midmark doing just that as she realizes the gift of wisdom from her mentors. Her knowledge is the currency of tomorrow.

Is your organization doing today what it will require to succeed tomorrow? Never forget, tomorrow is where you are going to live.

Nothing is forever. The future revolves just like the heavens. Today may appear to be standing still, but like the heavens, it is dynamic and moving. Markets have no memory and are not affected by your organization's biases. Markets can be cruel, but they are also real.

Author and lecturer Gary Hamel asks this question: "Are we creating a legacy or living off of a legacy?" As permanent as they seem, even bricks don't last.

This is another bit of wisdom from Yogi Berra: "The future ain't what it used to be." In his unrecognized wisdom, he is so very right, as things are moving at warp speed today, and I feel it will continue to accelerate.

Vision

The world runs on vision and those without it will always have to follow the ones who have it. Hockey great Wayne Gretzky said, "You must anticipate where the puck is going and be there when it arrives."

Every entrepreneur has a vision. Yet, they usually find that the original goal needs to be modified as no one is intelligent enough to see the total picture thoroughly. To bring the total vision into fruition, the entrepreneur needs team members who see the goal clearly, as well.

The vision must be so well understood, that *every* goal in the organization is aligned toward it. Toward that end, all the team members need to be involved in writing the vision statement, and it needs to be as brief as possible. Mission statements must be kept to four or five items to be effective. Mission statements hanging on the wall are fine, but unless each individual in your organization supports the mission statement, you might as well not have one.

The reason the vision is so important is that most people have some creativity within them, but sometimes it takes someone else's vision to bring it to the surface. That is very much a part of leadership. Look for what is missing, and ask, "What is it?" That allows creativity to come to the surface.

That untapped creativity need only be small steps that bring the vision closer to reality. Never forget that things like computers, xerography, or digital cameras were not one idea dropping out of the sky. It took teams of people with many creative ideas to bring the total concept to market.

Think big in your vision. Our CEO, Dr. Anne Eiting Klamar, openly states that she wants to build a billion dollar company. When I ask her if she is serious she says, "I want our people to think in those terms." Correspondingly, I feel you should think small in your operations (keep costs and expenses down).

Obviously, you can't change the past. Therefore, work on the future. To succeed dramatically, you must be able to draw knowledge from the unknown future and connect it to an economic success.

I've been cited as a clairvoyant or being able to see around corners. When I look back, that is certainly not untrue. My successes came from buying as much stock in Midmark (with total integrity) as I could afford, getting into the medical field while it was still in granular form, buying a home in Santa Barbara when California was in the tank, buying our headquarters plant and education center at low points, and getting into the digital industry early. Perhaps I was just a good buyer, but it does take a strong belief in one's self to do that.

I have taught myself to look for signs. A good example is my high school years. The course I liked best was economics. This has been my long suit in life. I look for tangible, economic signs, each one representing a star. If I find many stars in alignment, I see it as a *green light,* and that my financial decision will be a good one.

Success Keys

I'll take intelligence and guts over education anytime. Although we're staffed much differently today, we built a nine-figure organization with very few, if any, college degrees. Many times education can inhibit risk-taking. What is important is what you will learn, not what you know.

Having integrity when you are rich is much easier, but it's much more important to have it when you are poor!

It was Katharine Hepburn who said, "If you obey all the rules, you miss all the fun." Our people always agreed; "if we aren't having fun, we're doing it wrong!" And the more fun they had, the more successful we became. We did some very zany things in a very staid industry.

It is much more fun building your legacy than maintaining it. The thrill is definitely in the chase! (Which is why I always enjoyed finding and buying used Porsche Roadsters—it wasn't to save money, I just enjoyed the hunt.)

Be ambitious so your organization and people in it will be successful.

I always told our children, "If you only do 5 percent more than you are asked, you'll be very successful indeed!"

I also had the good fortune of having a lot of successful friends. Two of them were Tom Francis and Herb Schlater. They were in their 80s and I had the insight and good fortune to be able to ask them to a long lunch to get additional ingredients for this book. This is what I found that they had in common:

- Both started from nothing.
- Both had no formal education.
- Both were veterans of World War II.
- Both were religious.
- Both came from a big family and had big families.
- Both married smart spouses who were socially very adept and helpful and were very supportive of their businesses.
- Both had very solid marriages.
- Both worked hard but enjoyed what they did immensely.
- Both lived where they worked (walked the talk).
- Both never took success for granted; they appreciated their customers and employees.
- Both were very generous to charity; especially to their communities (you can give time, talent or treasure, and they gave to all three).
- Both could walk with the common man and when you spoke to them, you felt as if you were the only one in the room. They were very approachable.

"Today's sacrifices create tomorrow's success," said Bobby Knight, ex-basketball coach of Indiana University. "Everyone has the will to win. The difference is the will to prepare to win."

Find the toughest S.O.B.s in your industry and then go to work for them. Putting our *feet to the fire* is good for us all. What gets measured gets done.

Pareto's Law: This is important enough to write a full chapter on or perhaps even a book. It is the 80/20 rule, and I feel it fits *all* things in life. Essentially, it states that 80 percent of the time you wear 20 percent of your clothes, watch 20 percent of T.V. programs, read 20 percent of the paper and spend 80 percent of your time with 20 percent of your friends, and customers, etc.

From a business standpoint, you get 80 percent of your business from 20 percent of your customers, and thus, you had better be getting 80 percent of your profits. The same goes with 20 percent of your products. Thus spend 80 percent of your time, talent and money on that 20 percent and not on the 80 percent that is marginally profitable. That is called "Focus for Success!"

It is, in the long run, easier and faster to start from scratch rather than emulating something because to get to where you REALLY want to go, you won't have to erase first. Erasing drains off time, talent and treasure! Always start major moves with one line on a clean sheet of paper.

Finally, I have always found that the really successful people I've known were givers versus takers. I feel *giving* is the hallmark of a person who can think big and has vision.

PART NINE:
SUNSET

Succession Planning

The CEO should identify and begin mentoring their replacement ten years ahead of their exit. Replacing yourself successfully is the ultimate success story. Hire someone smarter than you, who is equipped to take the tasks at hand to the next level.

In a family business, the new president's big task is to take the business to a level that the old president could not. I was able to outdo my father. My daughter, Anne, our new president and CEO, in addition to already out-managing me, is smarter and more highly educated. I feel so fortunate that she is running the company. She has already *outdone me*.

In a family-owned company, unless your offspring are brighter, have better leadership qualities, have the passion and are vitally interested in leading the company…sell it! Otherwise, they will eventually destroy the company and ultimately their self-esteem with it.

But before you put up the For Sale sign, consider the benefits you are walking away from. Unless the company has become an albatross, consider bringing in a professional manager, sharing equity with them and simply have the family manage the results. This has been done very effectively and many times. Remember, you can only sell once and there is no turning back.

Your successor, whether family or not, may need to replace almost all of the previous officers. It is likely they cannot see the new president's vision or support it, and if they can't and don't, they will lose their job anyway as the company may ultimately fail.

Every organization has its own gestalt or persona. When it came time for me to leave, we at first brought in a third generation director to replace me as president. Even though he had been a director for eighteen years, after several years, our board of directors felt it was not working. It was extremely unfortunate for all parties. After a national search and vigorous testing, our daughter Anne was chosen as president. Her strong leadership skills and medical degree were big assets, and even though medical doctors generally don't understand business very well, she does. Why has it worked? Personally, I feel she deeply understands the culture of the company, its values and persona, and this gives her deep insight into its priorities and problems. Also important, she has passion in spades. She also feels the importance of doing well for our immediate and extended families.

It is vitally important that the successor has the courage to challenge the board chair. And the board chair had better be savvy enough to accept it without taking umbrage. The successor need not share the dream that the board chair has, because that person should have his or her own dream/vision which can inject new energy within the organization.

You can change leaders, but they had better have the same deep passion and beliefs. It is always better to promote a person to president who understands the fabric of the company, as decisions must be made with the *next generation* of management in mind. It also adds discipline because the time horizon of decisions, acquisitions, etc. must be multi-generational for at least twenty-five years. The weakest course for the business is for the leader to act like they'll live forever and leave the company equally to every child upon their death. Too, the children running the company should be able to buy out the children who are not involved, and the family member who is the leader has to have the greatest equity of anyone.

Succession is not a word but a process and a very complicated one at that. Be prepared to hand over the keys to the kingdom and keep your feelings to yourself. The successors will be more successful growing at their own pace.

The success of a private company depends on high-quality mentoring. Preparing yourself and the capable family member to be a successor is a lengthy transition while keeping the organization on track. Also, keep in mind the other family members who, though not capable, might want to be part of the company as well. Diplomacy is the key in a family company. It must be a win-win.

In 1967, I was elected general manager. At the time I knew nothing at all about management. In 1968 we located the product line of American Metal Furniture which we bought for $30,000 with borrowed capital. At the time, I didn't know a stethoscope from a crowbar. In 1969 I was the company's secretary, but not yet on the board of directors, and still didn't know how to spell *"general manager."*

At a board of directors' meeting that year, my father mentioned he would like to see me be president of the company someday. An outside director said, "What about right now?" The motion was made, a vote was taken, and I was president. Now how is that for long-range planning? I had just turned 32 years old. This was much too young by twenty years, but thanks to some wonderful people, I was able to handle the job. Fortunately, I already knew how to spell *"president."*

Retirement

I flunked it!

I was retired for about six months before being called back to work by the board of directors. I had moved my office into our home, and even our marriage was adjusting to my being on Esther's turf. My advice, however, and I quote Aloys Bertke, for whom I worked in high school, along with his son Norman: "If you retire, you had better have someplace to go."

Fortunately, I did. And even though it was back to Midmark part-time, I was all for it, as I feel strongly that you will rust out before you wear out. Correspondingly, push yourself both physically and mentally and push hard. Be manic about it! We stay *extremely* busy and just love it.

It is the furrows and repetitive patterns in life that weaken us. The mind is elastic and requires continuous stimulation in order to stay healthy. Be it computers, photography, volunteering or whatever; keep opening new avenues that challenge your thinking. One of the reasons we ended up in Santa Barbara, California, is for its stimulating atmosphere. We spend our winters there, continuing classes and lectures, from art to cooking. Naturally, my first love is business, and I lecture there at City College, Westmont College and I am also involved with the University of California.

Lecturing is wonderful for two reasons. First, many of the students are stimulating, but most important is the *giving back* of one's self to young, interested people. I can't give back to the people who mentored me (they need nothing) but I can give forward!

Retire *to* something meaningful, not simply *from* something.

The emotion of feeling needed for one's expertise is an element of a successful retirement. As a cautionary note, managers around you who say they are retiring in two to three years have a short-term focus and refuse to make the tough decisions that are required to move forward into the next decade and beyond.

One of our California distributors, Max Henlein, came to see us years ago when, I believe, he was 69. He was a wonderful man and friend, though now deceased. When our vice president asked him when he would retire his answer was, "Aw, Don, I'm too old to retire." He lived into his 90s.

My brother-in-law, Frank Brinkman, who was Midmark's CFO, decided to retire earlier than most, as he and my sister, Janice, loved golf and the social life in Florida. He played golf daily, but after a year or so he picked up a real estate license and was quite successful in the Florida market. He had a wonderful sense of humor and one of his golf buddies saw him at a store one day and quipped, "It is a shame some of us have to work." Never at a loss for words, Frank responded, "True, but at least now I can get an occasional day off!"

We recently had a director retire who was very successful in his career. I asked him what he would like as a token of appreciation for his fifteen years on the board of directors. The answer was, "I have everything and need nothing. I've gotten so many wall items I had to begin discarding them. So please give me nothing." Being in the same category, we began a program of planting a tree with a plaque for our retiring notables. He really appreciated that.

I once gave a graduating class talk called "The Four Seasons of Your Life." It went something like this:

Your spring consists of grammar, high school and college. Summer is starting your career, getting married, starting a family, making new friends, and buying a home.

Those two are your most important seasons. Hard work and good decisions are very important at that time. Your autumn hopefully finds you financially stable, your family raised, and everyone in good health. Winter can have its problems: Perhaps the loss of your mate, good health that is receding, and less energy to do the same things as in the past. But putting the four together, I think it creates a lyrical look at life, and summing it up, my favorite saying is still, "Life is good!"

Estate Planning

Estate planning is like the horizon. As you get closer to it, it continues to recede. This continuous movement is due to complexity and tax changes.

Get your children involved and start the initial thoughts and process at 47 years of age as we did. Surprises in estate planning rarely go over well. Never leave assets in your estate so they are co-owned by your offspring. You are only setting them up for disagreement and ultimately separation from each other. Correspondingly, ruling from the grave through trusts is a real platform for tension and unhappiness.

That goes for anything. Things need to be equal but not the same. To make things equal, one may get your home, while another might receive securities and cash, and another controlling interest in a business. Let this surface while you are good and healthy so you can arbitrate if need be. And really drive home the fact that businesses go two ways, up or down. There are no guarantees and ultimately an owner makes their own luck. It is not usually external.

Life is not a dress rehearsal. The best time to give love or money is now while you can see and enjoy the benefits. And, in addition to the charitable work Esther and I do, we feel the best investment we'll ever make is in our grandchildren's education. Now that is another win, win!

If you are fortunate enough to give your married children some financial stipends, make the check out to both husband and wife together. It will help bind their marriage and your combined relationship with your children and in-laws.

From Sam Walton: "The best way to reduce paying estate taxes is to give away your assets before they appreciate."

A snapshot of Midmark today...

Having just completed fifty years with Midmark, I remain Chair, but our oldest daughter Anne Eiting Klamar, a physician, is CEO and a very strong one at that!

The company, which was founded in 1915 by others, is financially strong, private, and we have no thoughts of selling. We are headquartered in Versailles, Ohio, a town of 2,500 people, and we have subsidiaries in Tampa, Florida; Gardena, California; Glasgow, Kentucky; Lincolnshire, Illinois; Ernee, France and a partner in Mumbai, India.

As a nine-figure company, we have positions in the medical, dental, veterinarian and digital diagnostic markets. Dr. Klamar's vision is "efficient patient care," and everything we do is toward that end. I will also add that we consider companion animals as our patients as well.

In its entire history, Midmark has made twelve acquisitions of varying sizes. Acquiring and assimilating is one of our "core competencies," and we intend to continue. Our strong suit seems to be niche markets.

Midmark has had two epiphanies. The first was going into the medical industry in 1969 as a metals company that made medical equipment. The second was when Dr. Klamar became president/CEO and changed what is *under the hood*. Thanks to her leadership and her husband's knowledge, we are now a true medical company. Midmark is governed by a very professional board of directors who reside in various states and represent different specialties. Three of them hold doctorate degrees. At the end of the day, we feel we are a somewhat *storied*, deep cultured company.

Esther and I and the Klamar family at the Health Industry Distributors Association annual meeting in Chicago, 2005. Anne was awarded their Award of Distinction, their highest award. From left, Rob's father John Klamar, M.D. and his wife Cathy, Esther and Jim Eiting, Ann Eiting Klamar, M.D. and her husband Rob Klamar, M.D. Seated are their sons Christian (l) and Carl (r).

EPILOGUE

When my father died, I said to my mother, "How tragic that all that knowledge is gone."

So...I chronicled mine in the preceding pages.

Now you've seen my dots of knowledge, dots I've collected through life experience, reading, seminars, school, and mentors. I hope you can reach in and select and connect the dots that will help you in your personal and working life. May they help you as much as what I have learned from others who have helped me. I have been so very, very fortunate.

Finally, when all is said and done, you can say to yourself, "I made a difference!"

God speed and fair winds to all.

James A. Eiting and Anne Eiting Klamar when she was named President in 2000.
She was such a strong and bright leader the board chose her to be CEO in 2002.